THE BEST MOM
IS A HAPPY MOM

Stop Doing It All And
Be a Role Model for Your Kids

JOANN CROHN

For more information, email hello@noguiltmom.com

ISBN: 979-8-89694-985-5 - Ebook

ISBN: 979-8-89694-986-2 - Paperback

ISBN: 979-8-89694-987-9 - Hardcover)

CONTENTS

DOWNLOAD THE BOOK
BONUSES FREE!

Read This First

I hope that this book entertains you.

But, more than that, I want you to take action on what you learn.

That's why I created a book bonus pack with the
tools to help you implement what you learn.

Download it at **noguiltmom.com/bestmom**

INTRODUCTION

I spent Christmas of 2019 crying on the couch.

I felt none of the holiday joy. Instead I felt abandoned and completely overwhelmed.

December felt like a neverending whirlwind of balancing my work, shuttling my daughter to dance practice, watching holiday recitals, attending holiday events, buying all the gifts, making all the meals, coordinating with all the family members—the list was endless. And I felt like I did it completely alone.

It seemed like every time I planned something, my kids would say, "*This is booooring*," or "*I don't want to eat this. Can we order from DoorDash?*"

My husband had a ton of work stuff of his own, which I made space for him to do. I didn't question it, nor did I talk to him about it. Instead, I absorbed more. I wrapped up his dinners when he came home late. I entertained the kids so that he could finish something up. I took on all the grocery shopping, present buying, and present wrapping. By Christmas day, I couldn't keep up the facade anymore.

I felt broken, depleted, and angry, and I couldn't hold it together anymore. So after opening presents and eating breakfast, I collapsed on the couch in uncontrollable sobs.

Do you ever get into this pattern? You see how you can make things easier for other people, so you step in and do it, but pretty soon, you end up doing *everything*? And then you find yourself making snide remarks with this growing pile of resentment and anger inside you.

You're not alone in this. So many women live in that spiral. As women, we've been told that to be happy we have to:

- Be better organized,
- Set up better routines,
- Take more bubble baths.

But that's not it *at all*.

I tried all of those things—and while they helped a little, they didn't make me happy. So I started researching: How could I get my family to take on more so I wasn't stuck doing everything myself?

I consulted business and relationship books about accountability and communication. I started my own podcast where I could interview experts and ask questions directly. What I found was that it wasn't about task lists, chore charts, or becoming more productive. It came down to:

- communicating my thoughts and feelings in a way that invited cooperation and problem solving—instead of brush offs, "I'll do it later," and defensiveness.

- managing my own stress levels so that I didn't strongly react to my kids' inevitable meltdowns after school when they couldn't find anything to eat in a very full pantry and they were "soooooo hungry."

- making sure to keep my own goals a priority—and staying connected to what my goals were—so that I wouldn't feel like I was putting myself last.

- learning to say "no" and not spiraling into worry that the person I said no to would be mad at me.

It was a long process, but I figured it out.

As soon as I saw my stress level ease and my resentment disappear, I knew I had to share it.

Now, I teach women to communicate more effectively with their kids and partners through my business No Guilt Mom. For the past eleven years, I've helped thousands of women to clarify exactly what they want and effectively balance that with the demands of motherhood and the social expectations that we've placed on ourselves.

Here's what women have told me after working through these changes:

- They're no longer losing their temper when their child spills something on the floor or strews all their toys across the recently cleaned living room.

- Their family is stepping up in the house with shared chore responsibilities so it's not just on them anymore.

- If they're in a partnership, they feel more supported. They're parenting together now—not doing it all on their own.

By the end of this book, you'll have the same tools they do. I've held nothing back. You'll be able to lower your stress levels, actually understand your kids and what they want, and step into a bigger life. You won't need to wait for anyone's permission (or for your kids to get older to do what you want to do).

Before we dive in, here's a heads-up: As you read, you may be tempted to put down this book and say, "*No. I don't have time for this now. I'll do this when I'm less busy.*" I get it. But I urge you to get started on what little you can now.

Often, we think that we need to commit a ton of time and energy to achieve the things we want. We need to clear our calendar and "make it a priority." But our lives rarely allow that to happen. Instead, try shifting that thought to: "*What's one small thing I can do right now?*"

The rough draft of this book took me six months to write. Four of those months consisted of me waking up, telling myself I *should* work on this book, and then never "finding the time." Things finally changed when I got so sick of feeling like I was letting myself down at the end of the day.

I kept telling everyone I was working on a book, and yet never sat down to write. So, I started a little accountability group in my Balance community called Body Doubling, where every morning at 6:00 a.m., I committed to show up for their work time—and mine.

We all jumped on Zoom. At the beginning of the hour, each woman announced what they would be working on, then we turned off our audio and video in order to work. At the end of fifty minutes, we jumped back on and reported what we did. In one month, the rough draft was done.

What's amazing is the women I led benefited too! They:

- focused on work projects they'd been putting off,

- tackled rooms they said they would declutter months ago,

- made serious progress in an online course, and

- finally found the time to meditate and exercise.

All because we made a consistent, small commitment of time to focus on something that none of us ever thought we had the time for.

Waiting only stretches the stress you're already feeling. It might take less time than you think. It's not other people or time holding you back from doing the things that you want to do—it's *you*. Not you as a person per se, but your beliefs about who you are and what other people think of you are preventing you from taking that next step in changing your communication and focusing on what you want.

Throughout this book, you'll be giving yourself permission to change and counter those beliefs. Each chapter will cover a different belief that's holding you back.

You're not alone in this anymore. Your frustration, resentment, and rage are valid. Today, you start giving yourself permission to live your best life—without guilt. Because friend, that relationship is about to get a whole lot better, too! The first step is becoming clear about what is stressing you out instead of trying to diminish it or push it down. So often, we're told to be grateful, and in the process, invalidate our own feelings about what's happening.

That's what we'll explore in Chapter 1.

"I Should Be Grateful All the Time."

When we as moms first have a kid, everyone around us is so excited. They say things like, "Oh, they're so cute! You're so lucky!" Family and friends get so excited about your upcoming child's arrival into the world, but few talk about how taxing and demanding being a parent can be.

We have two situations that can co-exist at the same time: being grateful and also completely hating some steps of the process. When you're allowed to recognize both, you can take the actions you need to feel good as a parent. If you don't, fear will take over, and that emotion will be the driver of your decisions. Such was the case for me when my daughter was born.

THE HOSPITAL

My husband promised he would only be gone for an hour. He was going to run back to the house, check on the dog, and get ready for our return home. It should've been a happy time. But as he closed the door of my hospital room, all I felt was fear.

"Oh my god, what have we done?" I whispered. My three-day-old daughter lay asleep on my chest. My post c-section meds had worn off and all I could think of was that I was alone and fully responsible for this incredibly helpless being.

I couldn't move very much on my own—as I had had a c-section. I was already exhausted and we were only three days in. What had I actually signed up for? How was I going to do this? I tried slowing my breathing. I tried calming down—my husband would be back soon, and before long, we'd all be home together. But nothing seemed to help.

When we finally got home, home didn't help. If anything, the panic got worse.

I was only a year into a career I absolutely loved—teaching—and I couldn't see how I could ever go back to work. How could I ever trust that my baby would be ok without me? How could something so fragile ever survive if someone didn't have eyes on her every second? I couldn't stop the thoughts that at any second she could stop breathing, and I knew that would devastate me.

I tried to smile. I tried to say, "Yes, I am so thrilled to be a mom." But the fear of losing her was too much. I couldn't enjoy motherhood at all. And because of that fear, I felt I needed to sacrifice every ounce of myself to protect her.

One month in, sleep deprived and no less panicked, I looked down at her and thought, "Only five years until she's in school. What if she's sick and I have to call out and get a sub? I'll have no control then, either. And then high school and driving. Then college. I'm going to be completely consumed for the next eighteen years. More than eighteen years, but at least at eighteen she'll be living on her own. Only eighteen years until my life becomes my own again. I can do this."

And then I broke down crying again. Was this normal? Was this just "baby blues?"

At my six-week postpartum appointment, my OB/GYN asked me, "How often are you crying?"

I answered, "Every day, sometimes three to four times a day."

She followed that up with, "And how's your sleep?"

"Not great," I said. "I can't relax enough to fall asleep. I keep picturing her breathing stopping in her bassinet next to me, so I'm constantly poking my head over to make sure she's still breathing. Then I panic because I think I don't see her chest moving, so I place my hand on top of her. That sometimes wakes her up, and I'm back to getting her to sleep again."

My doctor saw my signs of intense fear and, thankfully, referred me to therapy.

Looking back, there was a big sign that I needed additional help. I wasn't sleeping even when someone else was watching my child. My body was in constant hyperalert.

Are you in that state now? Where you can't rest, relax or even sleep—even when you're alone and your kids are taken care of? That is a clue that you may need help figuring out exactly what's going on.

Come with me to therapy.

FIRST TIME AT THERAPY

I pulled into the dusty gravel driveway of my therapist's home, nestled in a quiet ranch-style neighborhood on the outskirts of Tempe. It was one of those rare communities where each property was a solid acre and had horse stables in the backyard. It felt odd that this was a doctor's office. Her office, a cozy addition to the side of the house, looked more like a guest casita than a traditional clinic.

I removed my daughter's car seat from the backseat—unclipping it from the base and cradling the handle in the crook of my arm while balancing the seat on my hip. The car seat was heavy, but the stroller that it snapped into was practically the size of a small SUV, and there was no way I was dealing with that today.

Sharon, my therapist, opened the door and led us into her small office—white block walls, cool tile floors, and a soft, well-worn rug under a forest green couch that looked like it had seen its share of patients. The space had a lived-in feel, a little like my old Girl Scout leader's living room, which instantly made me more comfortable. I took a seat on the couch and laid my sleeping daughter beside me.

Sharon asked me how it was going and I said, "Fine."

"Tell me more about 'fine,'" she said gently.

"Well," I said, "I'm pretty tired. But, I'm surviving. My sleep is all off because I can't relax. My husband is helping with nighttime feedings to give me time to rest, but I can't even sleep during that time because I feel like I should be doing something too. I'm on edge all the time and even right now I just feel like crying." Which I did. I started crying right there.

Without further prompting, I started explaining one of the hardest parts of new motherhood for me: breastfeeding. I dreaded it—and it felt like it took up 85 percent of my life. I would sit down on the red couch in my living room and position her little head to latch. Getting a hungry infant to latch is not an easy thing. She would turn her head from side to side looking for the nipple. I would look for that big "O" her mouth made and latch her onto one side.

The first few seconds were like razor blades attacking my breast. I'd take a deep breath and slam my opposite foot against the coffee table to deal with the pain silently and not disturb this feeding baby on my other side.

Later, I discovered that was not how it was supposed to feel and we were likely dealing with other issues, like a poor latch. But at the time, I thought this agony was unavoidable and that was just how breastfeeding was. I found the whole experience painful and stressful, which—guess what?—also impacts your milk supply.

So I wasn't producing enough for her, and it would take her twenty painful minutes on each breast to get her fill. Then, I would get a forty-five-minute break before we started the whole process again.

Sharon took this all in and asked me, "If you don't like it, why are you still breastfeeding?"

"Because I have to," I replied. "Breast is best."

In the hospital, my room had this large poster by the door that said, "Breast is Best." Even the formula ads in 2008 had the disclaimer, "Breast is best, but ..." It all made me think that if I didn't give her breastmilk, I would be putting her at a disadvantage for the rest of her life.

My more pernicious way of thinking was that somehow breastmilk was this magical cure against all maladies, and she would get a horrible disease and die if I didn't make this sacrifice now. This would just be the first in a long line of painful sacrifices. I needed to give her my entire life, my comfort, and my everything.

Sharon then said something that changed my entire outlook—something that helped me break through my postpartum anxiety and depression.

"JoAnn, your only responsibility is to feed your child. That's it. It doesn't matter how you feed her. Just feed her."

I tried to fight her on it. I told her about what I heard in my prenatal class, how breast milk is magical and protects infants from disease. I told her about the poster in the hospital room.

But she remained steady. "No. All you need to do is feed her."

This wasn't the first time I heard this. I remembered something from my last doctor's appointment. The nurse handed me a sheet of paper. "Just in case you decide that breastfeeding isn't working,

I want you to have options," she said. The sheet explained how to stop breastfeeding if I chose to. I'd thanked her, then immediately dismissed the possibility.

But for the first time, there on Sharon's couch, I considered what my life would be like if *anyone* could give my daughter a bottle. If I could be free of pain. If I could sleep through the night. If I got my time back. If I got my body back.

My shoulders relaxed. I realized, for the first time, that I wouldn't be a bad mom for making that decision. I would, in fact, be able to be a *better* mom if I wasn't in pain all the time. That realization felt fantastic.

You are not a bad mom because you dislike some part of parenthood. The best mom is a happy mom. Your happiness is important. Remember, you can be two things at once: grateful to be a parent and also mad as hell at some parenting tasks. Getting clear on what exactly is stressing you and making you unhappy prepares you to take the next steps.

I left that appointment and went straight to the grocery store, where I bought a head of cabbage and some formula.

When I got home, I found a sports bra and stuffed in two fresh cabbage leaves. Then I dumped a scoop of formula into a bottle, filled it to the line with water, shook it up, and sat down on the couch to feed my daughter. For the first time, I felt relaxed feeding her. I was in control—and I enjoyed it.

Changing this one thing opened the door for everything else. I now wanted to go on a walk outside. I had the energy for that. I was able to start taking anti-depressants since she was no longer getting my milk. I was able to drink wine again, which I very much enjoy. Just one little mindshift changed my entire outlook. And it can change yours too.

HOW TO BE A GOOD MOM

Let me make a guess: you're reading this book right now because you want to be a good mom, but motherhood feels draining to you. You're wracked with guilt when you think of doing things that make you happy. And even if you wanted to do them, you feel like there's no time.

You've probably read parenting books about how to fix every kid behavior. You're trying to add more self-care into your life—but maybe it just doesn't help.

Recently, on an episode of "Armchair Expert," Dr. Mary Claire Haver, a menopause expert, mentioned how physicians used to over pathologize menopause. As a well-woman physician, if a woman had heart palpitations, she'd refer them to a cardiologist. Frozen shoulder? Off to an orthopedic surgeon. All along the true problem was hormones.[1]

In the same vein, I think that we over pathologize motherhood. We seek to treat all the symptoms of a larger problem.

Kids not going to bed? Cut screen time. Oh, and you're giving them too much sugar. Stop that.

You're screaming at your kids? It's because you're not taking enough time for yourself. More self-care.

---

1   Dr. Mary Claire Haver, guest, *Armchair Expert, "Mary Claire Haver,"* March 19, 2025, 10 min., 30 sec., https://armchairexpertpod.com/pods/mary-claire-haver.

Gained forty pounds? You're not eating right. You should fix that.

What is the larger problem? It's the rising expectations on women: how they spend their time, and what "being a good mother" is supposed to look like.

And, let's say it, the patriarchy. If you're not familiar with the phrase, the patriarchy is a belief that men are treated differently than women. It goes both directions where men are expected to sacrifice everything for work and women are expected to sacrifice everything for home.

Erica Djossa of MomWell says it best,

> "The current system often sets mothers up for failure. Mothers are expected to meet unrealistic ideals and shoulder immense unpaid labor, only to be blamed when they fall short...."[2]

I tell you this to say there is nothing wrong with you. This is not your fault. You are trying your best in a toxic environment.

Remember how I said that two seemingly opposite things can exist at once? You are in a difficult setting, but that doesn't mean you have to stay a victim in it. You have the power to change how you feel and thrive.

THE BEST WAY TO THRIVE IN MOTHERHOOD

Sixteen years ago, I started building a simple framework—one that gently but powerfully helps untangle so many of the challenges we face in motherhood. At its core, it's about making *you* stronger. Not by piling on more tasks or expecting perfection, but by nurturing your roots.

2   Erica Djossa, Email to author, July 16, 2025.

It's called the Lotus Framework. We're going to go deep into this, but let's start with the short version:

- Gain clarity on your struggles and where they come from.

- Calm your body through mindset work, physical activity, and finding joy.

- Improve your communication with your kids to get a deeper understanding of how they feel, while expressing how you feel.

- Claim a huge goal for yourself that excites you and is separate from your family.

- Strengthen your boundaries to protect everything you have created.

Imagine a lotus flower. From the surface, it seems to float effortlessly—serene, balanced, unbothered. But what you don't see is what lies beneath: a deep connection to the muddy bottom of the pond through strong, grounded roots.

That flower didn't just appear. It started in the muck—buried in the messy, uncertain, and unseen—and slowly, steadily pushed its way up through the water. It reached the surface whole and bloomed. Just like you can.

This framework isn't about fixing everything around you. It's about helping you rise while being strong, steady, and grounded, no matter how murky the water gets. Many women connect deeply with this metaphor because it reminds them that no matter *how painful their past* or *how overwhelming motherhood has felt*, they still have the power to rise. They can emerge strong and whole—a beautiful flower blooming above it all.

Think of this lotus flower as having five petals. **The first petal** represents everything you've been through, as well as your current challenges. **The second petal** represents how you feel, the stress that grows inside you. All of the terrible and complex emotions lying just under the surface that you're unaware of, yet they guide you day-to-day. These things cause you to hold onto imaginary rules, just like I did with breastfeeding.

I recently saw a cartoon that organizational psychologist Adam Grant shared on social media, and wow, it hit home. It compared how procrastinators and non-procrastinators approach rest and work. The non-procrastinator simply moved from rest into getting things done—calm, direct, no drama.

But the procrastinator? Instead of truly resting, they spent part of their downtime *worrying* about the work ahead. The result was less actual rest, and more stress—all before even starting the task. You do this when you fall into mom guilt. You worry about everything you should be doing—organizing, cleaning, prepping—until you rob yourself of the rest you need. That stress spikes your cortisol and wreaks havoc on your hormones and body.

The first step is noticing we're doing this to ourselves. The second is doing something that actively relieves that stress. I call this your Mind, Body, Unicorn Time. It means recognizing your mental patterns, moving your body in a way that feels good, and doing something fun—just for you.

The third petal represents what you hear and what you say. This is your communication. Many moms tell me their kids don't listen. But usually, the problem runs deeper. Unless you've taken a negotiation class, chances are no one's ever taught you how to communicate in a way that isn't about winning, but about finding a solution that works for everyone.

I was an eighties/nineties child and the style of parenting then was "listen to me or you're grounded." I turned my anger at the unfairness inward, thinking I was the bad one. It kept me in line. My sister turned it outward and raged when being told what to do.

Because of how your parents raised you, you may use the same parenting style toward your kids and then wonder why they don't listen. We assume we know why they're acting out—then wonder why they push back.

In the Netflix series, *Running Point*, Max Greenfield's character, Les, tells Kate Hudson's Isla, "You just don't care about me."

Isla was under a lot of stress running a basketball team, and I thought, "Oooh, that's just unfair."

We do this all the time as humans—we assume we know what others are thinking and why they act the way they do, without ever pausing to ask or understand.

In this book, I will teach you the skill of questioning in pursuit of understanding and curiosity. Once you learn this skill, you'll find that your child's behaviors start making sense, and when they don't make sense, your kids will feel safe coming to you after the fact to explain. This takes some time, but it's something you have to look forward to!

The fourth petal represents what you see for yourself in your future. As a group, women often lose their identities in motherhood. We cling to being "wife" or "mom" and forget to nurture the version of ourselves that existed before kids. It's not on purpose! I teach this concept and still fall victim to it.

My daughter got her driver's licence a few months ago. Now, instead of me accompanying her to drop her off at school activities and friend's houses, she drives herself. I found myself with open stretches of time that I thought I would relish, but instead felt this fear and emptiness. I often thought, "Holy crap, what do I do with myself?"

Eve Rodsky, in her books *Fair Play* and *Find Your Unicorn Space,* calls these outward goals, "Unicorn Space." It's the hobbies and activities that make you an interesting person outside of your roles of partner, parent, and professional.

For me, I started pilates, took up mountain biking, and I've chosen right now to write a book. That's not a coincidence.

These four elements represented by the petals: your past, how you feel, what you say and hear, and what you see for yourself, all need to be protected.

A lotus flower is protected by the water surrounding it. That's why **the fifth petal** represents boundaries, but boundaries are tricky.

I don't know about you, but I was raised to be a "good girl" who was cooperative and helped the people around her—all the makings of a people pleaser. It's hard to say no if I know that person I'm saying no to will be upset and unhappy.

This becomes insidious when you have kids and their job is to ask you for everything in the world, regardless of how ridiculous it may be. I found myself neglecting my own needs to satisfy theirs, which is great when you need to keep a newborn alive, but not as productive when your eleven-year-old wants candy at the airport.

TAKE ACTION

Throughout this book, I'll encourage you to take small actions at the end of each chapter. I promise they won't be time-consuming—and I'll always explain why they matter. Even though I'm a people pleaser, I also tend to rebel when people tell me what to do. So I'll present my case and let you make the final decision. Deal?

I want you to start seeing how these concepts might apply to your life and how you may be able to use them to thrive in motherhood. So, I have a simple reflection exercise for you. Feel free to either write these answers in a notebook or voice-record them in your phone's notes app.

First, think of a specific situation in your life right now that you're feeling a fair amount of stress about. Perhaps it's your kids' attitude. Every time you ask them to do their laundry, they sulk and moan. They tell you they're "fine" wearing dirty clothes and "no one notices, Mom." This starts a fight, back and forth, until your child stomps to the washer, throws their clothes in, and slams their bedroom door.

Or maybe your partner isn't noticing what needs to be done in the house, leaving you the one responsible for absolutely everything. He offers to help sometimes, but it always seems up to you to tell him what to do. You want an equal partner, not another person in the house to manage.

Or maybe it's a mother-in-law who criticizes your parenting. She goes against what you want for your kids—taking responsibility for chores, putting their clothes away—and thinks that a child's job is to play while moms do everything.

Write this specific situation down. While I'm typically averse to writing things down when told, I've noticed that when I do, it helps me get clear on what's actually upsetting me—and that makes the problem easier to solve.

Now, answer these questions:

1. How can you release the stress you feel immediately after this situation occurs? Think in terms of moving your body, writing it out, or maybe going on a walk with your dog.

2. What do you dream of doing in this situation? I think of how I wanted to quit nursing, but I wouldn't let myself. Do you have a thought of what you want to do, but think you would be judged for doing?

3. Is it possible that there is more information about the situation that you haven't found yet? Think of the other things that might be bothering your child/spouse/other.

By relieving your immediate stress, gaining clarity, and getting curious, you're on your way to writing your own permission slip to do what you want with your life.

PERMISSION SLIP

Give yourself permission to recognize the tasks of parenting that you don't like to do without shaming yourself for being a "bad mom".

Let's keep going and dive deeper into your triggers.

CHAPTER 2

"I Can't Stop Myself From Yelling."

Moms often tell me they can't stop yelling at their kids because the words slip out before they even realize it's happening. It feels out of their control, but it isn't. The key isn't forcing yourself to manage emotions in the heat of the moment; it's the groundwork you lay beforehand that gives you the calm and control you need when those moments come.

I'm known for wanting my way. Some may call it bossy. I like to call it determined. When I was younger, my parents used to call me "Queenie" because of this trait. I knew what I wanted and how I wanted it. I had a vision.

But as I got older, that same vision and clarity started to cost me friendships. People pulled away. During my freshman year of college, I took a road trip to San Francisco with three of my friends from the dorms: Alison, Nicole and Colleen. It was a fourteen-hour road trip from Arizona State. We drove to Santa Barbara the first night and then on to San Francisco the next day.

After we checked into our motel, we rested, unpacked, and then decided to explore the city.

This was 2001, way before smart phones. This was the era of looking up where you were going on Mapquest and then carrying a paper printout of the directions, which we purposely didn't do. We wanted to explore.

We left our motel and started walking toward what we thought was Fisherman's Wharf—down a winding, deserted street that seemed to lead into an industrial area. I hate streets like that—completely desolate, with no one around to witness my inevitable kidnapping.

I like to think I have a pretty good sense of direction. I'm not perfect by any means. I admit, now in the age of Google Maps, I don't even try to figure out north from south or east from west. I'll walk a block in the wrong direction before realizing the icon is moving opposite of where I intended—and then make everyone turn around—but it's rarely more than a block. Please don't ask my husband about the time I made him walk five miles to get chocolate truffles. That was a situation when I miscalculated the distance, but case in point, we were going the right way.

That night in San Francisco, I knew we were not going the right way. We were headed into a desolate, dark area—one where every sense in my body told me to run.

I said, "Hey, I don't think it's this way. I think we made a wrong turn."

Colleen, who was leading us, replied, "No, let's just keep going."

Five minutes later, I spoke up again, "I think we're going in the wrong direction."

Colleen stopped, turned and yelled at me, "JoAnn! You don't always know everything!"

That phrase hit me deep. As a nineteen-year-old, I had not experienced much conflict in my life. My entire life so far rested on knowing that if I was making people happy, I was doing the right thing. Toxic, I know.

I stood there and then felt the tears come. I bailed. I pivoted, said something like, "Fine, you keep going. I'm going back." I headed back up the hill to the main road.

Colleen followed and apologized, but I wouldn't talk to her, because I didn't want to turn into a blubbering mess over something so seemingly innocuous. I hated that her statement made me cry. I wished I was stronger than that. I thought at the time that because she hurt me, she deserved every bit of silence I gave her, but looking back now, I realize that I was triggered.

And she was triggered too, by what, I'm not sure. We didn't talk about those things.

She touched a tender spot in me—one I didn't fully understand at the time. It was the part of me that carried quiet shame simply for wanting what I wanted.

If you've ever felt this, you know there's more to it. There's that extra layer, the voice inside whispering that you're being selfish, that you're not thinking enough about everyone else's needs. Selfishness is one of my trigger buttons. It makes my emotions rise to an uncontrollable level if I'm unaware that the button has been pushed.

For me, this trigger shows up frequently in motherhood. For instance, when I want to rest but my child pleads to play a game with me. I feel like I'm a horrible mom for refusing, and yet I am resentful if I force myself to take part. When I say no, the littlest pushback from my kid causes a huge emotional reaction within me because I'm triggered when I'm presumed to be selfish. Can you relate?

With triggers, you can expect one of four typical reactions:

- Fight: You start yelling and try to hurt the person, probably verbally, in relation to the threat.

- Flight: You run and avoid the threat. This is my first instinct with every threatening situation, just like I did with Colleen. I run as fast as I can.

- Fawn: You bend to the threat's will. This would be like me saying, "Yes, Colleen, whatever you say." If you fawn, it doesn't mean you're weak. Typically, this behavior has kept you safe against aggressors in the past.

- Freeze: You're at a loss for what to do so you remain frozen and indecisive.

But it's not just the physical response you need to take into account with triggers. It's what you say to yourself in the danger, and the damage that you can do to yourself mentally. Since I don't fight on the outside, the battle happens in my head—I berate myself.

If you do this too, I've got a simple exercise that helped me understand where it was coming from.

CIRCLE THINKING

After I had my daughter, I was diagnosed with anxiety and depression. I've been seeing therapists on and off ever since, more than fifteen years now.

In those sessions, I've learned techniques that work for me, and I've taught others because they're so helpful. Once, I told my therapist how I could be in a great mood, and then, just an hour later, feel irritated and mad at everyone.

She told me, "JoAnn, you were triggered. The trick is to find what triggered you so that you can be on the lookout for it in the future."

You rarely catch your trigger in the moment before it has the time to affect your behavior, like yelling at a five-year-old for dropping his Cinnamon Toast Crunch on the floor. You find it by reflecting on the situation later using this strategy.

I first used this during afternoons when my son was two and my daughter was six. By the time 4:00 p.m. hit, I felt depleted, emotionally spent, and ready to lay down and cry into a glass of red wine. It's also when my mood turned on me the fastest. I could be happy and laughing, and then moody and depressed in less than five seconds.

Later on in the evening, I pulled out my journal and thought back to the exact time that shift happened.

1. Figure out the event.

It was when I asked my son to go pick up his Paw Patrol toys scattered on the living room floor and he replied, "No!"

My son was two. He said "no" at least sixty-five times a day. It wasn't the no itself—it was what I told myself after it.

2. Recall your thoughts.

Usually I thought, "Ugh, my husband is at work. He doesn't have to deal with this." Then I'd get mad at him. Mad at my decision to quit teaching and start a business so I could be "flexible."

Mad at myself for having kids at the beginning of a career that needed all my energy, because there was *no way* I could be as successful as I wanted to be and still be a mom. Since I couldn't be mad at my child and since I fully accepted responsibility that I agreed to all of this, I took it out on myself.

"JoAnn, you weren't such a great teacher anyways."

"JoAnn, you can't even get your kid to listen to you."

"JoAnn, if you had been eating healthy and working out, you wouldn't be so tired."

I was very, *very* mean.

It wasn't my son refusing to pick up toys, it was what I was saying to myself.

3. Ask yourself what emotion those thoughts caused.

The way I spoke to myself, I would *never* speak that harshly to anyone else. Not even close.

Those thoughts created feelings of regret, guilt, and shame.

What's the difference between guilt and shame? Guilt says you did a bad thing. Shame says that you're a bad and flawed person.

Shame is harder to recover from than guilt. "Mom guilt" should really be called "mom shame," because if you're anything like me, I bet there's a part of you that believes you're not cut out for motherhood, that you're failing at it every single day.

This is the strategy to lift yourself up out of this shame landfill.

4. Identify your reaction as a result of those emotions.

For me, the shame I felt caused an immediate decrease in energy. I no longer wanted to make dinner. I wanted to grab that bag of Swedish Fish I had hidden behind the cans in the pantry and eat my feelings.

This led to a whole other set of problems—like a stomach ache, and the urge to just scroll my phone while my kids watched endless episodes of *Fresh Beat Band* and *Peppa Pig*. While there's no shame in watching those shows, watching them because I was wallowing in a pit of shame was not good. I wanted to avoid feeling like a dumpster fire, but how?

5. Ask yourself, how can I change my thoughts to ones that feel better to me?

I'm careful about how I word this kind of advice. I think it's dangerous to classify emotions as either positive or negative. Especially as a woman, I feel the pressure to be positive as frequently as possible, and I think that emotions that don't feel comfortable fulfill an important purpose.

As Tera Wages, CEO of Connection Codes, says, "Joy isn't always a positive emotion. People flirt with a coworker because it brings them joy. I can eat a whole pan of brownies because it brings me joy."[3]

Joy doesn't always mean good. But, having those uncomfortable emotions, every day at the same time, when I'm taking care of my kids, made every afternoon harder—particularly if I was in a cycle of depressive thinking.

Let's break down and discuss one of the thoughts I had: "JoAnn, you weren't such a great teacher anyways."

This one cut deep and targeted my life choices for the past five years, as well as my general competence. I can't turn it completely around because that would feel inauthentic, but I can say: "JoAnn, you enjoyed being around your students and seeing them achieve great things."

6. Identify the emotions you feel when you tell yourself this new statement.

Saying my revised thought made me feel hopeful. It focused on what I could control and didn't dwell on the past.

When I said that to myself, I didn't go down an inner shame spiral. I instead had space to take a deep breath and move on.

---

3   Tera Wages (CEO, Connection Codes), "8 Simple Words That Can End Family Fights," *No Guilt Mom Podcast*, July 1, 2025, interview by JoAnn Crohn and Brie Tucker.

MAKE IT A PRACTICE

Telling yourself you'll never remember to do that in the moment is okay. It's totally normal. Trying to change your thoughts mid-meltdown isn't realistic. You've been running the same thought pattern for so long, it's become a habit.

Think of changing your thoughts and reactions like walking in a path of fresh, deep snow on the way to the mailbox. The first time, you have to lift each leg up high and stomp the snow down. It's slow-going and takes a lot of work. When you walk back to your house, you take the same path and it's a bit easier. Then, when you travel that path over and over, all that snow compacts and it becomes much less effort to travel to and from the mailbox.

This is your brain when jumping to shame-filled thoughts. You're so used to going down that path—or, in this case, neural pathway—that you're going from event to thought in a fraction of a second. Accessing thoughts that are more helpful is going to take effort and time because you're stomping down a new neural pathway—your new path in the snow.

You'll have to train for this one outside of the moment before you'll start seeing success when you're in the situation. Fortunately, that's what you can do when you take yourself through this circle thinking strategy when your emotions have calmed and you're better rested.

Think of the last time your emotions felt out of control, or simply when you went from content to angry. Take yourself through the circle thinking strategy.

To practice circle thinking, you must identify the:

- **Event**: What happened that triggered you?

- **Thought**: What did you immediately think about yourself or the situation?

- **Emotion:** What emotion did these thoughts cause? (Pro tip: If you have a hard time pinpointing the actual emotion, it may be easier to pinpoint your physical sensations. Do you have a tight throat? Are you nauseous? Feeling like you have a head rush?)

Then, change the thought. What's a more helpful thought that you can replace the previous thought with?

Notice the emotion. What emotion or physical sensation(s) do you feel with the new thought?

Give yourself permission to feel angry in the moment and forgive yourself for the reactions that you don't yet have control over.

Now, let's dive into how you get more control over your emotions through three simple habits.

CHAPTER 3

"I'm Selfish."

Ever feel that you're neglecting some of your basic needs to take care of others? Perhaps you're in this endless cycle of responding to a dish dropping in the kitchen or the dog peeing on the rug that you never have a moment to reflect. Or you put off that workout you planned to do because your kids won't leave you alone.

If, like me, you neglect these things because you feel selfish for continuing to want them when your kids need you more, this chapter will introduce a simple solution called Mind, Body, Unicorn Time.

This isn't something I ever talked about much, but it shaped how I learned to think about my body. When I was seventeen, I struggled with an eating disorder. While the behaviors eventually stopped, I don't think I ever fully healed the thought patterns that led me there in the first place. I won't go into specifics, but I can say that it was spurred by this overwhelming desire to be thin. Thinness was positioned as acceptance. As a kid who felt like the odd one out, I thought that being thin would help me have more friends and be happier.

At the time, I wanted to act and I was in a community theater production of *The Crucible*.

I thought that if I could control my size, I wouldn't be as vulnerable on that stage. Others wouldn't judge me. The audience would like me.

These thought patterns continued until I became a mom. We went to visit my in-laws in Minnesota with my daughter who was then a one-year-old. I saw a picture of myself standing by the lake and I absolutely hated my body. I decided right then that I never wanted my daughter to see me criticize myself in that way. I went to Weight Watchers, lost twenty pounds, and thought that was that.

That belief—that being smaller would make me more acceptable—never fully left. It just morphed.

Two years ago, I wanted to lose ten pounds, but I didn't want to simply be thin; I wanted to be strong, too. I absorbed all the messages from Instagram and news sources saying that "strong is the new thin." Being strong is now what would make me likeable.

My morning workouts centered around Peloton, and during my free time I scrolled through fitness Facebook groups, looking at before and after pictures of these now strong, fit women. Every transformational photo subliminally broadcasted that something was missing in them before. They looked happy in their "after" photos. Joyful. In control.

I thought I could fix whatever was wrong with me by losing weight. I felt uncomfortable in everyday life. My clothes didn't fit exactly right and I was pulling and adjusting my tops and jeans whenever I sat down. I'd be so focused on the roll of fat at my midsection that I couldn't fully concentrate on conversations, since I thought that that person would see it too and silently judge me.

I hired a diet coach and started counting macros. I'd have protein oatmeal in the morning, tuna mixed with cottage cheese and pickles for a snack, protein shakes and meals heavy in lean meats and veggies.

It wasn't a bad diet, and call me crazy, but tuna and cottage cheese is delicious together. My meal choices made me feel physically great. My pants started feeling looser. I could think more clearly. Emotionally though, the restrictiveness was hard to handle. I said no to cookies and full-fat ice cream. My kids and I like to eat froyo or Dairy Queen for a "sweet treat," and I said no to all of those. I missed that.

I could feel every bit of the deprivation. Each time I wanted something and told myself, "No, grab that pack of tuna instead," I felt like a child being told to eat the veggies with no dessert.

I remember watching the Netflix show, *Sweet Magnolias,* and this image of a buttery, flaky berry pie slice filled the screen and I thought, "I would gladly weigh four hundred pounds for that pie right now. At least I would be happy." This is such a normal longing when you're depriving yourself of something. You think that if you just stick to this strict framework, you'll hit all your goals. You just have to be strong. But that restrictiveness is never a long-term solution.

When I hit my weight goal, I relaxed my diet and refused to step on the scale. I felt relief and the freedom now to do what I wanted. I ordered sweet treats with my kids—four-pack boxes of Crumbl cookies with flavors like Twix, Oreo, and red velvet. We drove through the Dairy Queen drive-thru to get mini blizzards. We laughed. We had fun. We'd sit around our kitchen counter eating cookies, simply enjoying each other with no other goal.

I stayed away from the scale, and that stress that I felt so acutely about what I ate disappeared. It was the absence of dread I hadn't realized I carried.

Around Christmas, I noticed that my pants fit snuggly and I couldn't button a few of my old pairs.

Curious, I stepped back on the scale. I had gained twenty pounds. In my twenties, I would have retreated into a pit of shame, calling myself names like "lazy," "ugly," and "irresponsible."

When I looked at the number now, I was shocked at what came next. I didn't feel any shame. Every time I glanced in the mirror, I thought I looked pretty. Strong. Vibrant. And while I could compare pictures and videos of myself when I was thinner to how I was now and did admit there was a difference, I thought the much slimmer me appeared gaunt and too thin.

What changed? I hadn't gained much muscle, I assure you. Rather, my mindset had changed. I started a practice—that I now teach my Balance members—I wish I would have known sooner.

MIND, BODY, UNICORN

All the self-care strategies I've come across stress me out. While I would love to meditate, be constantly nice to myself, and repeat the same affirmations, I can't keep them all straight. I find that the practice that keeps me centered and healthy comes down to Mind, Body, Unicorn. This isn't another rigid morning routine. It's just a simple practice I actually stick to.

Let's break it down into its components.

Mind

The mind component consists of becoming aware of your thoughts. Similar to what we talked about in the previous chapter about not knowing the thoughts that take you from content to angry—we are generally unaware of many of our thought patterns. The secret to this is journaling, and trust me, I didn't take to journaling easily.

I'm the girl who has half a dozen new and beautiful journals with six pages written in each and 95 percent of the book blank. I would start, get bored and then abandon it.

Then, I read the book *How to Have Fun* by Catherine Price and had the opportunity to interview her for the *No Guilt Mom Podcast*. One big part of her book stood out to me. She talked about a practice she did each night with this phonebook sized planner/journal. In it she wrote the good things that happened during the day.

Each night, I noticed I was focusing on everything I hadn't finished. Total defeat. So I started writing down my wins instead. I felt lighter. Proud. Then, when I reviewed my week and saw all the wins stacked up, I realized that I had done a lot that week, way more than I had previously given myself credit for.

If you have one takeaway from this book, start writing down your wins. You will notice a marked improvement in your mood and outlook.

After my wins, I started writing just a stream of consciousness. I typically started with an uncomfortable emotion and either vented, acknowledged, or tried to soothe that feeling. I didn't gloss over anything. I didn't dwell, I just let all the words come out, and when I was done, I felt like I had processed my emotion. I knew what caused it and how to describe what I was feeling.

> For example, if I was feeling shame for bingeing on half a pack of Oreos, I would say: "I'm feeling ashamed right now. The Oreos tasted so good, but I felt nauseous after eating them.

> "I was bored and hurting and telling myself I was a failure. I used the Oreos to soothe an emotion, like so many other people do as well. I was in pain with those emotions. But, it's okay. I can't say it won't happen again, but at least now I know what caused it."

Never had I gotten that benefit from journaling before. That clarity helped me figure out how fixated I was on food and led me to the decision to ditch my dieting. That's when Mind, Body, Unicorn started to take shape.

When you journal this way, you're not just recounting your day. You're examining your feelings about what happened and why you may have taken certain actions, such as yelling at your child or eating an entire pack of Oreos.

BODY

If you grew up in the nineties like me, you probably have a very tough relationship with body image and exercise.

I'm an athlete. I'm happier when I'm active. I've run four marathons, am currently obsessed with Pilates, and coach my son's mountain biking team. But I also tend to swing to extremes. If I'm running three miles regularly, I feel like a superhero. If I skip a few days, I tell myself I'm a lazy slob.

Do you think in extremes like that, too? Perhaps you were in a PE class in middle school that made you run the entire mile, and any walking was bright with a heavy dose of shame. Maybe you read magazines like *Seventeen* that showed stars' workout routines, and they were so incredibly thin. You read in the article that they ran five miles a day and you thought, "Well, that's what I have to do too." And perhaps also like me, you now find yourself dreading any exercise you have to do. You are always happy after you workout, but getting there is a struggle.

Let me let you in on a secret: That's a sign that you don't actually want to do it. You don't find it fun, or at least enjoyable enough. There is absolutely nothing wrong with you. You aren't lazy. You aren't undisciplined. You simply haven't found a way to move your body that works for you.

I want you to start over with movement. I want you to find the fun in moving your body again. Like when you were a kid and you wanted to climb all over the playground. Up and down the slide. Playing tag. That's the energy you're looking for.

But here's the problem: In today's world, there aren't many spaces for adults to play. And maybe the places that are to "play," you're not into (I'm looking at you, pickleball). For me, any sport with a ball demotivates me. I'm too hard on myself during it as I find I possess no natural grace with hand-eye coordination, and so the whole ordeal is simply not fun. Making myself go and practice isn't any fun either, so I accept that I will never get good at pickleball unless I have some unique urge to start playing.

If you're giving yourself a hard time about not doing an easily accessible activity, you don't have to do it. But I want to ask you, "Is there anything you've been wanting to try that you've talked yourself out of?" Maybe you've given excuses such as:

- I'll try yoga after I lose twenty pounds so I can fit into cute workout clothes.

- I'll try rock climbing as soon as I can afford it (do you have an actual number?).

- I'm too old to…

These excuses are giving you a powerful indication that you need to go and try the damn thing! It's something that you want and your Bob (your inner critic. I'll tell you more about him later) is trying to keep you safe by making you not do it. Bob doesn't want to see you hurt. Bob doesn't want to see you disappointed.

There's a Pilates studio next to my business P.O. Box. I walked by it for months, watching women glide gracefully on the reformer. It looked elegant—and intimidating. I had so many excuses: I'll be klutzy. I won't fit in. I'll hate it. I'll be called a Pilates princess. All of my excuses were fear-based. (And spoiler alert: none of those things actually happened.)

To grow, you need to act *before* you feel fully confident. I finally acted despite the fear when my sixteen-year-old daughter told me she wanted to try Pilates. Since I was obviously considering it, I signed up for an intro class with her as something fun we could do together.

I walked into a class led by Vickie, an almost seventy-year-old, incredibly fit, ray of sunshine who is now one of my favorite instructors. I lay down on the reformer, put my feet on the foot bar, and had a huge smile on my face the whole class. I signed up for the next class on the spot.

Now I go to three or four Pilates classes each week, and I look forward to each one. There are moments when I feel like my core is on fire, or my IT band is going to snap, but for the most part, I really like it. I found the movement for me. But it wouldn't have happened if I didn't push past those excuses and try it out.

If committing to something right away isn't for you or you're not sure what to even commit to, start small with just ten-minutes of movement. You can try:

- YouTube yoga
- Dog walks
- Stretching videos
- Biking
- A walk around your block

This is about joy and strength, not weight loss. You don't have to lose a pound to feel strong. You're just having fun with movement. As you become stronger, you'll be ready to take on bigger challenges, if that's for you.

For me, I haven't lost a single pound doing Pilates. But, as I was getting dressed this morning, I noticed my thigh had a perfectly gorgeous muscular shape to it. I turned to my husband, "Wooo!! Feel this! Rock hard!"

He felt my thigh and then in his typical nonchalant way told me, "Yep, good job."

UNICORN TIME

In her book, *Fair Play*, Eve Rodsky introduces the concept of Unicorn Space.[4] Unicorn Space is that sacred amount of time that is dedicated only to you where you're not fulfilling one of your roles as a parent, partner, or professional. It's an activity that brings you joy and makes you an interesting person.

I'm sure you've had conversations with other moms and all you can think to talk about is your kids. I was that mom too. My days were so consumed with feeding, napping, and diaper changing. As toddlers, the discussion turned to napping, feeding, and potty training. When they reached school age, it was still feeding, sleeping, plus screen time and *all the activities*.

We're wired to protect our kids, but modern motherhood has taken that to extremes. In 1981, the high-profile abduction and murder of six-year-old Adam Walsh changed everything. Before that, moms were encouraged to foster independence. Afterward, fear set in and the cultural message shifted: A good mom always knows where her kid is.

That event happened decades ago, but the fear lives on. "What if something happens?" becomes "It'll be my fault." And that guilt? It hijacks your joy.

You've reached the point where even imagining free time to do something just for you feels heavy. Instead of joy, you may feel guilt that you're neglecting your role as a "good mother."

I got you. Just like with moving your body, I want you to start small. You can't walk into Neiman Marcus for a pair of $100 underwear after

4   Eve Rodsky, *Fair Play* (Random House, 2019), 258.

shopping at Walmart your entire life. You're going to feel awful. You have to work your way up to it. Maybe instead of Neiman Marcus for La Perla, you go to Victoria's Secret first. This is the same with Unicorn Space - something we refer to as Unicorn Time in our Balance community.

If you love art, but signing up for that art history class feels too big, start smaller. Go to a museum for an hour. Take one step toward what lights you up. That's how Unicorn Time builds—one choice at a time. This will help you work in your routine Unicorn Time.

It's okay if at first you can't think of how you want to spend your time. As women, we've been conditioned to put our own needs last and concentrate on the needs of our children. So many of us have done that for so long that we have no idea what we like to do. That's why it's so important to start now.

Our job as moms isn't to be needed forever. It's to work ourselves out of a job. Our kids need to rely on us less and less as they grow up so that they can thrive on their own. I'm feeling that now as my daughter just turned sixteen and has her license. I have large blocks of free time where I don't know what to do with myself.

If you're in the trenches right now with young kids, you may roll your eyes and say, "Wow, that sounds nice, JoAnn," and I assure you that I thought the same way when my kids were young. I used to watch the clock every afternoon with my body aching, so overwhelmed by noise that every minute past 6:00 p.m. that my husband didn't come through the garage door, I became angrier and angrier.

If you've forgotten what you like to do with your free time, it may feel more comfortable to drop something you planned to do, like write your book or declutter your house, than it does to put boundaries around that time and say no.

Your mind and body adjust to your situation. You may be stuck in a cycle of reactions instead of intentionally planning out what you really want to do. That's what leads us into this state where we forget who we are as people. Unicorn Time will bring that back for you.

To start, think about what you used to find fun before you had kids. Was it going to the movies? Acting in community theater? Playing an instrument? Hiking? Go find that person again.

My best friend and fellow No Guilt Mom work buddy, Brie, was able to find herself again right after her divorce. Her kids were eight and nine, and since she had a split custody arrangement with a week on and a week off, she had to find something to do with her time. She joined a singles group and tried all the things: going out for drinks, paddleboarding, discovering her love for live music again.

My friend Chelsea is going through a divorce now and starting this same transition.

But you don't need to go through a divorce or life crisis to discover these things. Start small now. Fifteen minutes is all it takes to get online and find an activity to sign up for. Pick something to try.

Two women closest to me show such great examples of this. My sister, Jamie, loves running and the running community. She created a group of women that do trail runs together. She has two kids who are currently one and six.

My sister-in-law, Melissa, embraced creativity and performing. She's joined a local improv group that she performs and creates with. Her sons are nine and six.

These women remind me—and I hope they remind you—that joy isn't selfish. It's necessary.

TAKE ACTION

Write to see how you feel, move your body, and go find your Unicorn Time to light yourself up. Start with small chunks of time if you feel that the guilt of leaving your family is so much that you won't enjoy your time.

You don't have to commit to anything major right now. You can:

- Try an easy exercise video on YouTube.
- Find and read a book about a subject that has always interested you.
- Start experimenting with writing your own stories.
- Take a one-session cooking, or Pilates, or pole dancing class (you never know!)

You might have some little thought nudging you that starts with, "I've always wanted to try ..." Follow that thread.

You have permission to go and focus on yourself.

Now that you're going to start trying activities just for you, you may have a big hurdle in front of you that's preventing you from moving forward. It's shame. Shame for how you lost your temper in the past or reacted to a family situation can keep you stuck. You'll learn how to move forward from that in the next chapter.

CHAPTER 4

"I Feel So Much Shame for How I Reacted."

The feeling that everything falls on you is a heavy load to carry. Your mind is so filled with mental to-do lists that you have no space to think or decompress. When something unexpected happens, it's reasonable that you explode.

Maybe you spent the last thirty minutes straightening up the living room—putting your toddler's toys in baskets, wiping down the coffee table, arranging the pillows, vacuuming. Finally, you feel secure. There's less chaos. You exhale.

Your five-year-old comes in screaming and launches a toy at the television.

"What the hell are you doing?" you scream.

"Oh my gosh," you think. "What just happened? I swore at my child. What kind of parent am I?" I hear variations of this story from so many moms with the same concern: "I can't seem to stop myself before I react. What can I do?"

When you explode, it's not simply one thing you lose your cool over. Your five-year-old disturbing your well-organized peace is not an isolated incident. Rather, it is the take-out box on the top of a stuffed garbage bin that causes the entire thing to topple over.

STORMING DOWN MY BLOCK BAREFOOT

I want to share a moment when I reacted more strongly than I wish I had. I still carry some shame about it, but I also want to show you how I moved forward.

A few years ago, my sister came to visit me for the weekend with my then three-year-old nephew in tow. I was really excited to see her, but I could tell the entire weekend that there was tension lurking.

Like any righteous big sister, I disagreed with the way my sister viewed some situations. My nickname was Queenie growing up for good reasons. I thought my way was the right way and everyone else was wrong. I've learned to pull this inclination of mine back, but if I'm being honest, I'm still incredibly confident in why I do what I do. However, I'm aware now that this attitude has a negative effect on my relationships.

Every single person has a story driving their decisions that we're not aware of, and I need to humble myself that I probably only know 30 percent of the story. That weekend, I thought I knew the answer to all my sister's problems, and even though I thought I was being kind about it, it came across as a flat out rejection of all her choices.

The defining moment came in my kitchen. I had disagreed on a piece of advice that she had given my daughter, and I said, "Well, no, that's not right."

My sister responded, "You know what? Fine! I'm leaving. I don't have to take this!"

She called for her son and went to the guest room to pack. I should have let her calm down. I should have let myself calm down. But I didn't. I stormed after her, thinking I was being the rational one. That's when she said, "JoAnn, you always make me feel less-than."

And I—ever the emotionally evolved adult—shot back, "I can't *make* you feel anything."

Now I'm totally aware of how pretentious I came off saying this to another adult.

Then, she volleyed back and hit one of my personal triggers. "You know what, JoAnn, you don't know everything. You're not a doctor. Why don't you go back and get a degree?"

This was one of my biggest insecurities in my life, and still is in some respect. Even though I read voraciously in the psychology space and have been able to help moms stop letting guilt run their lives, I think that I'm a fraud because I don't have a Doctorate in Psychology.

This one hurt. This one hurt so bad that I immediately jumped in to defend myself and it sounded like: "F- you!" where I then slammed the door to the guest room, stomped to my own front door, and marched right out into the street—barefoot.

I reached the corner of my street before logic kicked in, "I am a grown adult. This is my own house. I'm not leaving my own house."

I marched right back and confronted my sister again. We didn't waste time. The yelling started almost immediately. We rehashed events that happened years ago that she was upset about, yelling at each other in front of our kids and my husband. It was not one of my proudest moments.

And then she gathered her son and walked out my front door. She blocked my number and social media. I cried. I texted her to apologize thirty minutes later, but she didn't get it. She cut off all contact for three months. It was the worst three months of my life.

During those three months, I was a little mad at her, but I was mostly mad at myself. I made a mistake and I couldn't correct it. I just had to deal with it.

At the time, I didn't have the understanding of my part in the issue like I do now. I now realize what I was doing, how I was treating her, and how upset, alone, and awful that must have felt. I do my best to correct that in every interaction I have with her to this day.

I don't regret the fight—not because I'm proud of it, but because it taught me what nothing else could. It was the wake-up call I needed.

The key to controlling your reactions is to make mistakes and then become deeply curious about why you made them.

If you're losing your temper when your child spills their cereal all over the floor or when they can't find their shoes, it's a clue to dig deeper. Here's how to do it.

REFLECT

You may feel like you need to apologize immediately. Don't yet. You're apologizing out of instinct, but you're not yet aware of why you did what you did. You need some time and perspective before that happens.

I came across this idea of emotional zones in *The Yes Brain: How to Cultivate Courage, Curiosity, and Resilience in Your Child* by Drs. Dan Siegel and Tina Payne Bryson.[5] They're kind of like a traffic light for our feelings—giving us simple ways to recognize what's going on inside and how we can respond.

When you are in the green zone, you're calm, thinking logically. All systems are go.

When you're in the yellow zone, you can feel the tension building in your body. Things are starting to annoy you. If one more thing goes wrong, you may just explode.

When you're in the red zone, you're apocalyptic. All of your logical thoughts have gone completely offline and you're acting from pure emotion. It's in your red zone that you scream at others and lose self-control. Recognizing these emotional zones helps you catch yourself before you explode—and makes it easier to come back from it when you do.

Before you apologize, you need to get back in your green zone so that you have access to the facts of the situation. As a kid, when you did

---

5   Daniel J. Siegel and Tina Payne Bryson, *The Yes Brain: How to Cultivate Courage, Curiosity, and Resilience in Your Child* (New York: Bantam Books, 2018), 34.

something wrong, you were probably taught to apologize. However, you likely were also never taught how to appropriately apologize.

Real apologies go beyond, "I'm sorry," or, "Well, I wouldn't have reacted that way if you didn't…" That's deflection, not accountability. A true apology takes full responsibility for your contribution. Yes, two people are always involved in a conflict, but when apologizing to your kids, as the adult with the fully formed brain, your job is to model the repair. That starts with reflecting on your part: What do you wish you had done differently? What caused your reaction?

When I was trying to apologize to my sister, I was in the yellow emotional zone—still stressed out, feeling a lot of shame, and wanting her to forgive me because I wanted that horrible feeling of her being mad at me to go away. It was not because I was ready to admit my contribution to the situation.

When you consider an apology, there's some nuance in these reflective questions that I want to explain.

What do you wish you had done differently?

In the fight with my sister, I wish I hadn't screamed "F-you" at her and slammed the door. I wish I could have noticed that the statement she said—"You aren't a doctor"—triggered me, and that I had removed myself from the situation right there.

Removing myself is something I'm able to do now about 80 percent of the time. When I notice I'm triggered by something my daughter says to me, I respond, "Okay," and I leave the room.

If I'm triggered in a situation I can't leave, say when I'm with my five-year-old nephew, I will make an excuse to give myself a little bit of distance, such as, "I need to go get something from the kitchen," or, "I'm going to go throw this away over there."

When I leave, I let all the feelings come. I'm a crier. All my emotions come right out of my eyes. Or I vent, either to my husband, my best friend, or if no one is available, my journal.

Sometimes I even start a new document on my computer and let all my emotions rage out as my fingers fly across the keyboard. Saying, "All the things about this situation are unfair. Why do I have to be the responsible, patient one, and why are other people such insensitive, unreflective fools?"

It's cathartic to say all the things alone that are considered taboo to say out loud.

What caused me to act the way I did?

When it's all out, then I'm able to come to grips with how I actually feel about the situation and what I may have been able to do differently to get a different outcome. I also get a lot more insight on what thoughts I was having at the time that caused me to react the way I did.

Any time you react in a way you're not proud of, something triggered you. Some internal thought process set you off on the path of fireworks and explosions. In the case of cleaning the living room, what were you thinking?

- I'm such a lazy ass, this living room shouldn't be as messy as it is.

- Why am I the only adult in this house who actually cleans up the living room?

- I hate living in this chaos or mess.

When you reflect in this way, you may realize that it's not actually your child you're mad at, but rather you feel this deep resentment toward your partner for not helping contain the mess. This reflection points the way to a bigger conversation that you need to have with them that you may have been avoiding. Don't worry, we'll get into those conversations later in the book.

APOLOGIZE

Once you've dug into the reasons and feel you're back in the green zone, you're ready to apologize.

Now, you may be thinking, "JoAnn, that other person is *way* more to blame than I am here. Why am I apologizing?" I'm not denying that. That may be very true. Apology isn't about taking blame. Rather, it's taking responsibility for your contribution to the situation.

That contribution could be something as simple as, "I should have said something sooner."

Even though the other person may have "started it" or been "unreasonable," stating your contribution immediately helps defuse the situation, and in most cases will then encourage the other person to state their own. This isn't always the case, though. Many people have not done the work that you're doing now, but this is your most reasonable chance at a reconciliation.

With kids, apologizing is super effective because not only are you communicating that you care about them and their feelings, but you're modeling how someone should apologize. Your child is going to expect that others treat them with respect because their parent has treated them with the same respect.

Kids also feel emotionally safe knowing that they are in the care of an adult who's aware of their mistakes and is actively working to improve them. In order to apologize, you must first calm down. Wait until you're in the green zone—because no good apology ever comes from the red zone. Then, own what you did. Not why. Not the reasons. Just the actions.

In the case of the fight with my sister, I had a lot that I could take responsibility for:

- Not noticing how my behavior was affecting her
- Screaming at her
- Slamming the door to the guest room

The list goes on. Were there real reasons I did each thing? Absolutely. But they don't belong in an apology.

I wish I would have handled myself differently. That's on me. I can take that on. Because once I apologize, we can both start to clear the air on exactly what went wrong, and take the steps necessary to fix it.

It could sound like:

> "I'm sorry for the way I reacted. I regret screaming at you and slamming the door to the bedroom. I also hear you when you say that I was telling you what to do, and I can see now how it could look that way."

I'm not taking responsibility for the entire fight by apologizing, simply paving the way for more discussion.

TAKE ACTION

Think of the last time that you reacted stronger than you would have liked. What do you wish you would have done differently in that interaction? Name it as your contribution, and if possible, apologize to whomever you need to.

If it's to your child, they are going to see you modeling how to make a mistake right. If it's to another adult, it may pave the way for a larger discussion with them admitting their contribution as well.

PERMISSION SLIP

You have permission to get mad. Our behavior is not always under our conscious control and you're reacting unknowingly to triggers that are buried deep. Being angry does not mean you're a bad person or that you should stay calmer and more grateful. It means you're human.

Noticing your contribution and telling others you're aware helps connect you to other people. Right now, if you're feeling lonely, connections might feel difficult. In the next chapter, you'll be working on how to connect more with others.

CHAPTER 5

"Nobody Cares About Me."

Ever catch yourself wishing someone, anyone, would check in on you first? Maybe you've waited for that text, that invite, that "How are you?" only to be met with silence. If, like me, you've realized that waiting leaves you feeling even more alone, this chapter will show you how taking the first step to reach out can open the door to the connections you've been craving.

Such as what I found when I had my first child.

"She never checks in or invites me anywhere," I told my therapist, feeling all my new-mom loneliness and frustration boil over. I felt trapped at home—RSV season meant the pediatrician advised keeping our newborn away from public places. And at twenty-seven, I was the first of my friends to have a baby. No one else was around during the day.

None of my friends understood what I was going through. They didn't know the isolation of new motherhood—how it swallows you whole. Still, one friend did have a kid, and at the time, I pinned all my loneliness on her. I wanted her to be more friendly, more nurturing, and see my obvious need and reach out to fix it.

My therapist listened and then told me another truth bomb that changed my life. She said: "JoAnn, the person who wants the change needs to be the one who makes it."

BE THE CHANGE

When she told me that, I was a little taken aback.

I thought, "You're my therapist. You're supposed to be on my side." But, she was right.

Looking back, I realize this friend had no idea I wanted to spend time with her—reaching out probably never even crossed her mind. And now that I understand her personality better, I can see she likely doesn't crave connection or social time in the same way I do.

I did end up reaching out, and we hung out once, which was really nice. But in the end, I realized I didn't need hours of hangout time to feel connected. She already had a close friend she spent time with, so the drive to create something new just wasn't as strong for her as it was for me.

That didn't matter though, because having the permission to go out and create these opportunities to spend time with others was really what I needed. I had low self-confidence in my teens and in college. You can call it shy—I call it extremely low self-worth. I believed everyone else had some magical quality I didn't. That they wouldn't want me around. That I'd be a burden.

Loneliness has a way of lying to you. I said "no" to myself before anyone else could say "no" to me.

In my mind, I rationalized that if I was invited somewhere it meant that they actually wanted me around. That's not true.

HOW DO YOU MAKE FRIENDS?

It used to be simple—standing around at pickup, chatting with other moms. Now, making friends as a mom feels like trying to start a conversation inside two separate moving vehicles that are at a stoplight for just a few moments while you're yelling through your closed car windows at each other.

I used to wait for my daughter after school on the playground. That time gave parents a chance to talk, connect, and share the small moments of raising kids in the same community. Then a new principal shut down public access, saying the school would be safer. Now we sit in our cars, lined up and isolated. And who can argue with safety? But that kind of safety makes us lonelier than ever.

How are we supposed to meet friends?

At our No Guilt Mom retreat in Cancun, a group of six women sat on a patio overlooking the Caribbean, sharing how painful it was when people assumed we were too busy and didn't invite us at all.

So many women find themselves caught in a modern version of the mommy wars. Moms who work outside the home aren't invited to playdates because stay-at-home moms assume they're too busy. Moms who work from home think the same thing about each other if their schedules don't align. Everyone assumes. No one reaches out.

It was easier when we were in school. Friendship was built into our day. Our friends were the people that we had physical proximity to. We ate lunch together, sat together in classes, and waited together after school for our parents to pick us up.

Now? It feels like a friendship desert. You're not alone if making friends feels harder than ever. I tell you all of this to reduce the shame you feel when you have to put more effort into finding friends. That doesn't mean connection is impossible. We just need new tactics. Remember what my therapist said: the person who wants the interaction needs to initiate. Yes, that means stepping outside our shy bubbles—where rejection feels terrifying—and making the first move.

Margarita Mondays

When I moved into my new neighborhood, I envisioned a close community—neighbors who knew each other's names, helped out when needed, and threw the kind of block parties I'd only heard about. My neighborhood did have a social committee with cookie walks, Easter egg hunts, and even a Turkey Trot—but I still barely knew anyone. I wanted to change that. So, on our neighborhood Facebook page, I made the first move. My post read:

> Hi! I would love to meet more of my neighbors! If anyone would like to come over on Monday at 5, I make a pretty awesome margarita. Let me know if you want to come.

At first, I got a few likes but no RSVPs. As an entrepreneur, I've learned that the fortune is in the follow-up. So I messaged the people who liked the post and others I'd met casually through neighborhood events or dog walks.

I got a few yeses and a whole lot of, "Maybe, if I can make it."

On the day of, I received a few last minute back-outs (always to be expected) and then at 5:00 p.m., I sat in my clean kitchen, half-terrified that no one would come and the other half terrified that someone would.

At 5:30 p.m., the doorbell rang. It was Bethenney, who I had never met. Bethenney was a mom to young kids and coincidentally a physician's assistant at my gastro doctor's office. We sat on my back porch drinking margaritas. Then Jen, a yoga instructor, joined us. Then Julie. It was fun chatting and getting to know each other.

Then a month later, I hosted another get together which I called Tequila Tuesday—because yes to alliteration. This time my husband joined and we had more of a mix of women and men. Andi brought a huge charcuterie board. Julie brought watermelon margaritas, so we had two types of margaritas.

We talked about doing it again. No one followed through. But here's the thing—this chapter isn't about finding your forever best friends. It's about making the first move. I wanted to feel more connected in my neighborhood, and I do. That's enough. Planning a monthly event is a huge commitment, which I was happy to do for a short time because I needed the interaction.

I'm not ruling out another margarita night; but for now, my friendship bucket is full.

HOW YOU CAN APPLY THIS

I wanted to tell you this story because when you initiate a friendship, it's not a lifelong contract—and it doesn't have to come with expectations. Sometimes you'll click and grow closer. Other times, you'll be at different stages and simply won't have much in common. But you'll never know unless you take the first step.

So what can you do next?

Since you're looking for people like you, plan something you genuinely enjoy. I love margaritas—but also books, movies, and adventure. I might invite friends to go to a movie or start a book club.

A local shop near me lets groups make their own candles after hours—it's BYOB, and all they ask is that everyone buys their candle. See? It doesn't have to be elaborate. Just pick something and do it.

Know that other people are lonely too

I worried no one would want to come, or worse—that I was inconveniencing my husband and kids. My own kids didn't even come out to say hi during Margarita Mondays. At fourteen and nine, they just wanted their space, and I worried I was damaging them by inviting people into it.

But me inviting people over has a ripple effect. It encourages my kids to invite friends over too. To take up space. To have an imperfect gathering where the only thing you prepare is a few sodas and a bag of potato chips. To be able to be the house in which their friends feel safe, welcome, and respected means a lot.

It's not just your kids that deserve it, you deserve it, too.

Just like you might be wishing for someone to invite you out so you don't have to be the one making all the plans, there are others out there feeling the exact same way. But here's the upside: When you're the one who takes the initiative, you get to choose the place and the vibe. That means you can pick something that truly feels fun and fulfilling for *you*.

What if I have nothing to say?

My first career after graduating college was in the entertainment industry. I moved out to Los Angeles and got a job as an assistant to an agent at one of the major talent agencies, Endeavor.

One of the primary jobs of an assistant is to network, which means a lot of after-work drinks. I knew how important it was to network, but I was painfully shy and absolutely hated it. I was the person who would always cancel drinks at the last minute with the excuse that I wasn't feeling well (I was fine) or my boss needed me to work (he didn't). I would just rather spend the evening with my cats than in some bar with expensive drinks and forced conversation.

I thought that if people I talked to on the phone all the time met in person, they would be unimpressed and may even doubt my ability to work in this industry. So I said "no" to myself and made up an excuse. It was Bob—my inner critic—showing up again and again. He kept me very safe, but he also impeded my growth.

What I found from years of pretending to be an extrovert was that I only needed a few tricks to get by. These will work for you too as you go out and meet people.

#1: Always have an "in"

If you're a bit socially anxious, like I am, the one thing you need to prepare is a strategy to insert yourself into any conversation.

At a recent conference, I found myself alone in a large group of people, waiting to get in. I had no one to talk to. I used to avoid these events and hoped and prayed that someone would come up to me and start a conversation. Typically, this plan never worked out, so I stayed in that corner and learned to hate parties.

But then I realized that being outgoing isn't a born trait, it was something I could learn. Vanessa Van Edwards studied these traits in charismatic people in her book *Captivate*, and broke them down into essential skills that anyone could put into practice.[6] One of these is developing your strategies in starting a conversation. My favorite strategy is to comment on what someone is wearing and give them a compliment.

At that conference, I was surrounded by men—pretty common in marketing. Since my business serves moms, I usually connect more with women. In a crowd of two-hundred, I spotted the only two women in the room. One wore a bright pink blazer. That was my in.

I walked up, stood beside them and introduced myself to both, "Hey, I'm JoAnn." Then I turned to her and said, "I love your pink blazer."

Was I interrupting? Absolutely! Did it matter? Not in that case. They welcomed me in and I joined the chat. What's cool is that these relationships lasted. One has become a collaborator and one of our podcast guests. The other has introduced me to phenomenal people.

Initiate! Interruption pays off.

6   Vanessa Van Edwards, *Captivate: The Science of Succeeding with People* (New York: Portfolio, 2017)

#2 Know how to continue

Now that you're in the conversation, what comes next?

As I mentioned before, I tend to be drawn to very bright colors. This is how I made friends with Erika Cartledge when I attended Mom 2.0. She was wearing a gorgeous pink jumpsuit. Continuing with my always reliable strategy of complimenting someone as an introduction, I walked up to her and said, "I love this color pink. It looks gorgeous on you!"

After she said, "Thanks," and told me where she got it, I asked her my standard follow-up: "Where are you from?" With the second question, I'm trying to find similarities between myself and them. It's a game I learned from Christina Hillsberg and her book *License to Parent*.

Christina and her husband, Ryan, used to work for the CIA and the technique, "You Me, Same Same" is a strategy used to develop an asset where you try to find similarities between yourself and whoever you're talking with[7]. This develops trust and commonalities which can be used to build a deeper relationship.

For example, a conversation can go like this:

Me: Where are you from?

You: I'm from Wyoming.

Me: Oh, I've never been to Wyoming. (This is my cue I need to find something else.) Are you streaming anything good right now on Netflix?

7   Christina Hillsberg, *License to Parent: How My Career as a Spy Helped Me Raise Resourceful, Self-Sufficient Kids* (New York: G.P. Putnam's Sons, 2021).

You: Yes! *Running Point* with Kate Hudson. I love that show!

Me: Me too! Same!

I found a similarity and now we have something to talk about.

When I was working in entertainment, I thought I had to read and memorize the entire *New York Times* to keep up. But I didn't need to sound smart—I just needed a few good questions to steer the conversation toward something we both enjoyed.

#3 Keep it going

When it comes to conversations and making friends, you need to know how to be a good conversation partner. Remember, this isn't an inherent skill, it's something you can learn, so stay with me here.

Ever get into those conversations where the other person dominates and you are stuck there nodding your head even though you're not interested in what they're saying? That's not the conversation partner we're going to be.

Alison Wood Brooks, a Harvard professor, teaches a class on how to have great conversations. In her book, *Talk*, she breaks it down into an acronym.[8] I recommend her entire book, but I'm going to focus on the "T"—topics—for now. Now, here's the shocking thing. So many people get overwhelmingly nervous when it comes to new conversations that they go blank and can't think of anything to talk about.

8 Allison Wood Brooks, *Talk: The Science of Conversation and the Art of Being Ourselves* (New York: Random House, 2024).

Before a social situation, Alison recommends that you create a list of topics. My question, "Where are you from?" is from the topic list I always choose from. The rest are:

- First memory as a kid
- Something coming up that they're excited about
- Where they most want to travel
- Their favorite place to travel/where they have traveled
- Favorite book they've read recently
- What series or movie they're watching right now

In my topic list, I'm looking for the "You Me, Same Same"—something that sparks my interest enough for me to continue the conversation and stay engaged.

Now, this may appear selfish, but remember that you're not doing the other person any harm in finding a topic that interests you, because by asking the questions, they're interested in it too.

Isn't it weird/intrusive to ask a lot of questions?

I used to think so, but I've found through practice that typically other people are just as nervous and awkward as I am and seem to love that someone else has taken an interest in their lives.

Amanda, one of our Balance members, was visiting London and chatting with a group of British friends. The friends wanted to know something about another person and pushed Amanda, the American, to make the approach and ask. "You're American," they told her, "No one will think poorly of you because being loud and outgoing is expected of you."

Yes, Americans do have a stereotype when it comes to their nature, and you may not feel like you fit the mold. I tell you this to say that you may be holding yourself back more than you need to if you're worried about appearing nosy and odd. Other people want to be this way too and feel held back by cultural standards. We're all dealing with something.

TAKE ACTION

The next time you're in a group where you don't know others well, practice these two strategies:

1. Introduce yourself by complimenting someone on something they're wearing.

2. Continue the conversation by asking questions and using the "You Me, Same Same" strategy by trying to find something you have in common. To reduce any anxiety you might have, write out a list of topics beforehand to prepare.

PERMISSION SLIP

You don't need people to show that they care about you by reaching out or making the first move. You have all the power within you to make these friendships without waiting.

The person who wants the interaction needs to make the first move. The first move doesn't need to be perfect. You're allowed to make mistakes. I'll teach you how to cope with those mistakes next.

CHAPTER 6

"I'm Not Consistent."

Do you ever berate yourself for not sticking with things? Then, maybe after beating yourself up, you end up quitting whatever you tried to start, since you couldn't be consistent? Consistency isn't the problem here. We're going to break down what is.

MARATHON TRAINING

When I was twenty-two, I decided I wanted to run a marathon, even though I didn't run. At all. I told everyone I hated running. I'd never gone farther than a 5K. So why a marathon? Honestly, I thought if I ran one, I'd finally lose the ten pounds I was holding onto, and everything in my life would magically click into place.

Then a flyer arrived: Train to End Stroke. If I raised $5,000 for the American Stroke Association, they'd train me—and send me to run a marathon in Kona, Hawaii. I went to the info session, equal parts excited and terrified. What if I couldn't raise the money? What if I couldn't even finish the race?

Coach Lori listened to my doubts and said, "You'll run a 10K on the way to a marathon. Might as well go for it now."

So I did.

At our first group run in Balboa Park in Encino, I stood among twenty people who all looked like much better runners than me. I tried to keep pace and only lasted ten minutes before I stopped to walk. I felt ashamed and questioned whether signing up for a marathon was my best idea.

Then, Coach Brian pulled up beside me on his bike. "That's okay," he said, "You're out here. You're up. Do it at your own pace."

That simple statement gave me the permission I needed. I walked most of that run. At the end of practice, the coaches handed out the training schedule which planned for five days of running each week. I had never run that much in my life.

I worked at a talent agency in Beverly Hills with a one-hour commute from my apartment each morning. Luckily, we had a very small gym in the complex with a treadmill. I set my alarm and went downstairs for my weekday runs at 5:00 a.m., where I never saw another soul.

The first run was thirty minutes and I thought, "Okay, I'll walk for a bit and then I'll run." Throughout the session, I berated myself.

"JoAnn, everyone else on the team is probably running this entire thing."

"JoAnn, just try a little harder."

"Why are you being so lazy? Can't you push yourself?"

But I finished, took the elevator upstairs, and showered.

I did that again and again. Always hearing that voice telling me I wasn't trying hard enough. The following week, I was able to run farther. I wasn't perfect, but I kept showing up.

I skipped a few runs during the week, but I did make the long group runs a priority. These were Saturday morning meet-ups where we ran an obscene distance. We started at six miles and worked our way up to twenty.

A month into the group runs, I ran the full twenty minutes to the turn around spot without stopping.

Two months in, I ran a full forty minutes.

Even Coach Brian noticed and called me out as most improved on the team.

When I stepped on the starting line at 5:30 a.m. in Kona, Hawaii, I didn't know how far I could make it. I wanted to keep running as long as possible, with only a thirty second walk break at each water station to hydrate.

I ran the first eight miles—eight miles! The woman who could only run ten minutes just a few months prior. After that, I fell into a run/walk pace, and then the last six miles were pure, hot torture as any first-time marathon runner can tell you.

I did it. I crossed the finish line in five hours and twenty-four minutes. I was a marathoner.

It wasn't a perfect training program. I could even make a case for not being consistent. But I lasted through training. Remember when I said that twenty people were at that first group run? Only ten of us made it through to the end.

Right now, your life may be co-opted by your kids' needs and you can practically guarantee that anything you plan to focus on, that focus will be pulled from time to time. You don't have to be perfect to make it. I need you to hear this, especially as a mom.

CONSISTENT DOESN'T MEAN WHAT YOU THINK IT DOES

The problem isn't that you're not consistent. The problem may actually be that:

- You're trying to do too many things at once, or
- The voice in your head berates you until you stop, or
- You can't get clear on exactly what you should be focusing on.

Remember how we talked about neural pathways in Chapter 1? It's stomping that path through the snow to the mailbox where at first it's really difficult and challenging, but as you traverse it more and more often, the snow packs down and it gets easier.

Now imagine that instead of one mailbox, you had ten and you had to go to a different one each day to get your mail. How fast would you expect it to get easier to carve a path to any one mailbox? Your progress would be much slower. You may not even see progress for a good three weeks because your effort is divided up between so many mailboxes. That's the difference between focused effort and scattered effort.

As a mom, you're forced to divide up your time. You probably have huge expectations that you should see progress faster, but you're not given that gift of *focus*.

Focus often requires support, resources, and relief from survival mode.

Katie, a mom of two in the Bay Area, used to work in Human Resources, but her passion had always been health. On the nudge of her boyfriend, she decided to quit her job and pursue health coaching full-time. Because she was a single mom of two teenage boys, she had a huge responsibility to provide for her kids. She couldn't have had the singular focus on health coaching without her boyfriend's belief in her and his financial support for the family. The gift of focus is huge.

I was able to focus on being a marathoner because I had no kids at the time. I was twenty-two. All I had to focus on was work, my boyfriend (now husband) who I lived with, and running.

If you're telling yourself that you're not succeeding because you're not consistent, it's an outright lie. You may not be succeeding because you have so many responsibilities that it's impossible to keep them straight.

But I'm not telling you this so that you throw your hands up in the air and forget it. I tell you this so you remember to be kind to yourself throughout whatever process you're struggling with right now.

MEN GET TO FOCUS

Men often get the gift of focus—but not because they're more disciplined. They get it because someone else handles the rest, usually a woman.

Kendra Adachi, author of *The Lazy Genius*, told us on the No Guilt Mom podcast that 92 percent of productivity books are written by men.[9] Men who don't have to coordinate carpool, call the dentist, or remember that the laundry still hasn't been folded.

Kaylee, a mom of two from Reno, Nevada, used to love photography. She took pictures in her free time, until one day her camera broke. As she was shopping for a new one, her now ex-husband told her she couldn't buy it, "it was way too expensive." So, she gave it up.

Kaylee didn't have the support needed for her focus. Ironically, her ex-husband—who discouraged her from spending money on a camera—picked up photography as a hobby himself.

Shanee, a pastry chef in Sacramento with two kids, has a very supportive partner—but she doesn't get to indulge in her favorite hobby: making elaborate cakes. Between all the sports practices, school activities, and being there for her family, she feels that making cakes adds on more stress and work. It goes from being something fun to something that stresses her out.

I've been there. When your hobby becomes one more thing on your massive to-do list, it ceases to bring joy and relaxation.

So what can you do about it? Before we get into action steps, we need to talk about the 4 C's.

THE 4 C'S

Marketing guru Dan Sullivan created a framework that every person can use for success in any area of their life. Whether it's trying a new parenting method, starting a new career, or pushing yourself past your

9 *Kendra Adachi (author and podcast host), No Guilt Mom Podcast, episode "How to Master Productivity (Even Though It Was Built for a Man's World)," October 15, 2024, No Guilt Mom*

comfort zone and doing something you've never done. He calls them the 4 C's: confidence, commitment, courage, and capability.

Many people think that you need to have all four to start something hard, but that's a misconception. You only need two: commitment and courage. Confidence and capability aren't necessary to begin; instead they're developed as you set out to achieve the thing you're trying to do.

Here's why: every meaningful endeavor is hard. My challenges won't be the same as yours—but hard is hard. What matters is having the courage to begin and the commitment to keep going, even when the path gets rough.

Courage to ask

Most women attempt to take on everything by themselves. Not only their work, but the work of those around them as well. When it gets to be too much, they'll most likely drop the project that meant the most to them personally. This is the recipe for burnout. Every time I do this, I turn into "Grumpy Jo"—the snarly, resentful version of me.

Here's an example. Every year, No Guilt Mom hosts the Happy Mom Summit. It's a weeklong event with over five thousand people attending online. During that week, I'm at my computer from 7:00 a.m. to 5:00 p.m., and I am *on*. I'm peppy on camera and reacting live to guests and putting out fires behind the scenes. It's exhilarating, but exhausting.

The first time I did it, I thought that I could handle all the other responsibilities I usually take care of, such as school pickup, making dinner, hanging out with my kids after school, plus the summit. Why did I do that? Why did I think I could just add on whatever extra activities in my life without any repercussions?

I did okay pushing through on the first day of the summit. But by the second day, I started to feel the resentment bubbling up inside me.

"Why isn't anyone else offering to help?"

"Why isn't my husband pushing his work schedule aside because he surely sees how stressed I am?"

Here's my wakeup call to JoAnn during that time. I want to tell to my past self: "Jo, only *you* push your own responsibilities aside and drop everything when you see someone else stressed."

Ouch. It's true.

I thought I was being selfish for asking for help in the first place, which is probably why I refused to clear my schedule prior to the event. I had to ask. I had to plan ahead. This may sound harsh, but it's an incredibly selfish thing to pile a ton of stuff on your plate and expect everyone to shift their schedules to give you a hand.

The next year, I started asking for help for summit week the month before.

I approached my husband, "Hey, summit week is coming up. I'm going to be exhausted and need your help. I need the most help with: making dinners, school drop-off, and school pickup. Can you help me figure out how we can cover those?"

With the advance notice, he put it in his schedule and took care of it. The resentment went away and was replaced by a deep appreciation for him.

Commitment to yourself

In my interviews with women for this book, a common theme emerged: we commit wholeheartedly to everyone else's needs—volunteering, chauffering kids, taking on work—but when it comes to our own needs, we fall short.

I'm guilty of this too. For an entire month, I didn't prioritize writing this book. I kept telling myself that I couldn't be unavailable—especially when my eleven-year-old son was home. He needed me to listen to him, right?

Then, at the end of the day, I had this gnawing feeling of guilt that I should have made time to write. That tiny relentless voice told me, "You didn't write again." It sat heavy in my stomach, turning every moment of relaxation into restlessness. I had made this "commitment" to myself and I wasn't following through. I couldn't decompress in the evening, and yet I couldn't drag myself off my phone to sit down at my computer and write.

But I had to write if I wanted a finished book.

I noticed that this was a problem for other women in our Balance program too, sitting down and actually doing the things that all of our good intentions wanted us to. How do we actually make it happen? I had an idea: body doubling.

If you're not familiar with body doubling, it's a great strategy particularly for those with ADHD. When you have trouble with focus, the entire world entices and distracts you. Body doubling means you sit down with another person who also needs to focus and concentrate on a separate, independent task. By working alongside one another, you keep each other accountable.

In Balance, we meet on Zoom and each work on our own projects. Right now as I write this, Brittany, a mom of three in Oklahoma, is getting in her core workout and walking two miles on the treadmill. Christy is feeding her chickens and then working on meal prep. Nancy is participating just by waking up and joining the call at 6:00 a.m. and then using the time to journal.

Commitment is simply about showing up at the time you've promised, no matter what. It doesn't require perfection or exceptional productivity. You don't have to be the most efficient or the most inspired—you just need to show up. Once you do, the momentum follows.

Confidence and capability aren't a given

You may have zero confidence in yourself and your abilities. That's okay. For the time being, you can borrow my confidence in you that you can succeed in whatever you want to do. I'm confident because I've seen it happen to thousands of people, both in my role as a coach and my experience as a teacher.

You have no idea what you're capable of because you haven't yet committed to showing up and working on it regularly. Confidence comes through sustained effort on a task, and I promise that you will see progress. You'll also discover what skills and knowledge you're lacking to complete your endeavor. That's expected and part of the process! Because what are you going to do? You're going to develop the knowledge and skills.

In one of our body doubling sessions, Christy planned to finally tackle a report she'd been putting off for work. But once she sat down, she realized something—she was missing key pieces of information. That discovery set off the next step. She had to reach out to coworkers, make a few phone calls, and gather additional details. Suddenly, the task wasn't a quick checkmark on her list, it was going to take more time.

She kicked herself for not starting sooner. But here's the thing: she wouldn't have *known* what she needed until she sat down and committed to the work. That's the whole point. You don't show up to be instantly perfect or wildly productive—you show up, uncover what's missing, and go get it.

Don't let your lack of confidence or the fear that you don't have the right skills hold you back from starting—because here's the truth: those skills and that confidence only come when you have the courage to start and keep showing up. And yes, I get it, some days you might feel so low, so defeated, that even showing up feels impossible. Or you make one tiny mistake and immediately think, "That's it! This is a sign I shouldn't be doing this. I'm doing too much." But those thoughts don't mean you're on the wrong path, they're simply part of the process you push through on the way to something bigger.

Showing up doesn't mean your execution will be perfect. You will make mistakes. Christy also experienced this during a body doubling session. Her goal for the hour was to meal prep for the week. During that hour, as she was chopping vegetables, her hand hit the cutting board and veggies flew everywhere. It was at that point that she would have usually given up, but since she was in the body doubling session and knew she would have to report to the group how she did, she picked up the veggies, cleaned up and started over.

As she reflected on the situation, she said that she usually falls into all-or-nothing thinking—where either it's perfect or "what's the use?" But she got the meal prep done, even with veggies flying all over the kitchen. Small recoveries count more than perfect execution.

HOW WE THINK ABOUT PROGRESS

As parents, we experience neverending to-do lists. If you measure your success by how short your list is, you'll feel like a failure every single day. Dan Sullivan and Dr. Ben Hardy, authors of *The Gap and the Gain,* offer a new perspective.[10] Instead of looking at your list and thinking how much you still have to do, measure it instead by where you started.

Think of standing outside your front door and looking at the horizon. As you start walking, you have this clear goal in sight and you're focused. However, will you ever reach that horizon? Absolutely not. That's not how horizons work! Our planet is round and it's physically impossible for you to ever reach it. If you measured the success of your walk by how close you get to the horizon, you would fail every single time.

This is the gap: the distance between where you are and where you want to be. When you focus on that gap, what feelings come up? Maybe defeat. Maybe discouragement. Maybe even a hopeless whisper that you'll never get there. It's not that you're not consistent. You're

10 Dan Sullivan and Benjamin Hardy, *The Gap and the Gain: The High Achievers' Guide to Happiness, Confidence, and Success* (Carlsbad, CA: Hay House, 2021).

placing your thinking in the wrong direction, which is making it hard to show up each day.

Now shift your focus. Think about your walk today and measure it from where you started—your own front door. You took steps. That's progress you didn't have yesterday. And that, my friend, is the gain.

When you think about the gain, what feelings arise? Accomplishment. Pride. Maybe even a little victory dance. You walked the same distance, did the same thing—yet the lens you choose changes everything. Focus on the gain, and you will feel uplifted. Focus on the gap, and you will sink into self-pity. So why not stay in the happy? Staying in the happy propels you forward. It boosts your self-worth and energy. And most importantly, it helps you show up for another day.

TAKE ACTION

Time to reframe a big goal you've been working toward, or maybe just your morning walk. Instead of thinking about the gap (how much you still have to do), think of the gain (how much you've already done).

PERMISSION SLIP

Give yourself permission to think differently about your progress. You get nothing from berating yourself over everything you didn't do.

Sometimes, what you still have ahead might scare you. I'll help you get through that next.

CHAPTER 7

"This Is Too Hard and Scary."

As a parent, some of your behavior may be driven by fear. You may be scared your child will get hurt, won't have what they need, or even become a horrible, narcissistic human being if you don't fix their behavior right now. I'm going to help you address that fear so it's the passenger instead of the driver.

In eighth grade, I was in a car accident. I was riding in the back of my friend Christina's mini van with her mom driving. They were taking me home after dance class and I remember looking forward at the road.

Then the world blurred—like an out-of-focus photo, or a painting smeared by a careless brush. I found myself on the floor of the van between the first row of seats and the sliding door. My nose was bleeding. I had not been wearing my seat belt. I honestly believed I'd see a crash coming. I thought I'd have time to react, maybe even buckle up at the last second. That belief shattered instantly.

We were driving south on a major road and someone tried to merge into traffic from a side street, but didn't see us. I felt the jolt, heard the crushing metal. He clipped the back of the mini van and the car spun 180 degrees.

My friend Christina had been turned around in her seat looking out the back window and she was now screaming, "Mom! My arm! There's something wrong with my arm!"

Fire trucks came. Paramedics came. I told them that I thought I buckled my seatbelt, but it must not have been in all the way (at that age I had a huge fear of getting in trouble).

Thankfully, everyone survived. However, Christina was out of school for a month. She needed surgery on her arm and dealt with lasting minor nerve damage.

I thought I was okay. And physically, I was. Mentally those scars stayed with me.

NO DRIVING WITH OTHER PEOPLE

After my childhood accident, I convinced myself that if anything happened to my kids in someone else's car, it would be my fault for being "too lazy to drive." That fear took over. I became the one who offered to drive everywhere. I was the girl scout troop leader, and who drove everyone? Me. When other people offered to help, I said, "No, I got it. I like driving."

Friend, I don't like driving. I was just absolutely terrified that my child would be in a car accident if I gave up that control. Every time someone offered to drive my kids or pick them up, I said no. It's funny how the things that happened to you as a child affect the way you parent.

My brother-in-law was the most adventurous kid. He jumped off things and raced fast cars, but then when he became a parent, he became shakily nervous when his four-year-old climbed something three feet off the ground.

Even the boldest risk-takers can become surprisingly anxious parents. We carry our scars into how we care. If you're struggling with fears and anxieties, know that it's not your fault. It may have a root cause in past experiences, and those don't just disappear.

I remember first experiencing anxiety at the age of ten. If my mom was late coming home from work, I would pace up and down the sidewalk of our house looking for her white Plymouth to come around the curve. This was before cell phones, so there was no simple phone call to be made. Typically she stopped at the store on her way home from work. My dad told me not to worry, because that's what you said to people then. As if the fear would magically go away.

"Oh," you say, "you told me not to worry. Yes, that helped. Worry is gone." Unfortunately, the brain doesn't work that way.

I was left to deal with that fear on my own, just like you may have been.

Dr. Russell Kennedy, author of the book *Anxiety RX*, recommends treating anxiety as if you're comforting and embracing yourself as a child.[11] The first time I used Dr. Kennedy's technique, I cried.

11 Russell Kennedy, *Anxiety Rx: A New Prescription for Anxiety Relief from the Doctor Who Created It* (St. Martins Essentials, 2024).

I pictured myself when I was ten-years old, standing there in my fluorescent lime and hot pink shorts, split color right down the middle, and imagined hugging myself just like I do my own kids.

I felt my ten-year-old hair cupped under my hand and the fabric of my t-shirt as I put a hand around my shoulders. I told myself, "It's ok to be scared right now," and I broke down crying. It's a powerful exercise. Your body keeps itself in cycles you may not be aware of.

THE QUARTERBACK VS. THE BENCHWARMER

Let's go back to neuroplasticity for a minute—the idea that your brain can change and grow based on what you practice. Remember the snowy mailbox path? Hard at first, easier over time. Let's build on that.

Think of your current anxious thoughts as a strong quarterback. He plays in every game and he has this down. He works out all the time, ready to crush his opponents because of how much practice time he's amassed. He's your anxious thoughts, running plays in your brain for years.

Compare him to the benchwarmer, who admittedly is a little weak. He has been to the gym perhaps once in the last week, and during practice sessions he sits out, just watching. This benchwarmer represents the calmer, more supportive thoughts that don't get much game time. Our job is to help the benchwarmer practice. That's it. He's not expected to go in and beat the quarterback immediately. He simply needs to start playing.

How can we let that calmer thought get the chance to step onto the field? We give him the chance to practice.

SELF-COMPASSION

How hard are you on yourself? If you're like me when I started working with my anxiety, I berated myself for being anxious. "C'mon JoAnn, this is holding you back. Why are you like this?" This internal thought process intensifies our anxiety. This self-criticism is common in Western societies. We mistakenly believe that if we're hard on ourselves and point out all the things we're doing wrong, we'll get better.

I like to call this voice "Bob." Bob means well. He's trying to keep you safe, but he does this by criticizing every new thing you do so you'll give up and leave. If we follow his lead, Bob causes us depression and greater anxiety. Being told repeatedly, even if just by yourself, how much of a failure you are doesn't release the happy thoughts.

Dr. Kristen Neff, author of the book *Self-Compassion*, knows what does.[12] She's been studying it extensively for years. The opposite of self-criticism is self-compassion, and it's much more than simply being kind to yourself. Self-compassion consists of three key parts: 1) recognize you're hurting, 2) know that you're not alone in your pain, and 3) comfort yourself.

1. Recognize you're hurting.

Here's something you probably haven't been told before: When you feel anxious, you're in pain. The first step of self-compassion is to acknowledge that pain. When I comforted myself as a child in that anxious moment, I finally gave myself something I never got growing up—comfort for my invisible pain. The kind of pain my parents couldn't see, just like yours probably wasn't seen either.

12 Kristin Neff, *Self-Compassion: The Proven Power of Being Kind to Yourself* (William Morrow Paperbacks, 2015).

When you're anxious and scared, you feel physical pain. Perhaps it manifests in the pit of your stomach, or as a closed-off throat, or possibly a headache. Maybe you feel a tightness in your chest. You are hurting at that moment. Denying the hurt doesn't take away the pain; it's giving that strong quarterback more practice time because you're criticizing yourself. This is a moment to let your benchwarmer in.

Recognize the pain. It's as simple as telling yourself, "I'm hurting right now."

2. Know that you're not alone in your pain.

In the practice of self-compassion, there's a concept known as "common humanity." Simply put, common humanity means that other people have experienced the same emotions and struggles that you have. Knowing you're not alone in your struggle, gives you the strength to push through because it takes away your self-critical tendency to think you have to do this by yourself. Shame is strong if you have anxiety, and shame thrives in isolation.

I can't tell you how many times I've compared myself to others who I thought had it all together. In high school, I was extremely cruel to myself when I didn't stay up late studying for whatever test was the next day. I called myself lazy, saying that I deserved my B. Did that help me stay up later? Absolutely not. I may have even gone to sleep earlier to wallow in my ineptitude.

I was comparing myself to my very studious friend, who was the anomaly. Instead, if I had thought about the dozens of other students in that class who I didn't know as well and thought about their study schedule, they may have been kicking themselves and worrying about not studying either.

When I went to my twenty year high school reunion and talked with some of these people, I was amazed at how many feelings and struggles we shared. It's common to put yourself in a box when you're a teen and think that you're the only one struggling. If you aren't intentional about removing this box as an adult, your benchwarmer will stay weak and never get any practice. Instead, calm that benchwarmer when he gets nervous. He doesn't have to perform at the same high level as the star quarterback. Other people are suffering too.

Another piece of common humanity is identifying that your anxiety doesn't live in isolation. There are many more events that led up to your eventual reaction. For example, when I was pacing up and down the front sidewalk of my house worried about my mom, I was already feeling unsettled. I was nervous about a book report that was due that I had been putting off. My little sister (seven years younger than me) was probably following me around and getting in my stuff. There are many things that happened that led to that reaction. It wasn't just me "being anxious."

When you acknowledge that, you're able to treat yourself with a little more understanding and kindness so that the benchwarmer can get some playing time.

3. Comfort yourself.

How often do you take the time to soothe yourself? To wrap yourself in comfort until you feel better? I have a tendency to push and grind, many times gaslighting my own pain and discomfort and thinking that it's all in my head.

You don't need to simply endure it when you're in pain, just like you wouldn't push your child to struggle through pain. Instead, do something simple to soothe yourself. This can be curling up in your softest blanket and reading fiction on your couch, or it could be something small you can do in the moment, such as taking a few deep breaths, or stroking your arm.

HOW SELF-COMPASSION HELPS YOU DO HARD THINGS

We know logically that as parents, our kids grow up and need to learn how to navigate the world on their own. A lot of the new things they need to master feel intensely scary to us. So scary that we step in to overprotect and restrict.

Case in point: when my son first rode his bike next to a busy street, my husband and I went through all the steps we could to protect him.

Helmet: check.

Husband in front, me in back: check.

Choosing a street with wide bike lanes: check.

But I was still nervous. However, I was also conscious that my nerves and anxiety could pass along to my child. I didn't want him to be afraid of biking. I turned to self-compassion to calm myself.

As we turned onto the busy street and I watched my eight-year-old pedal in front of me, I first acknowledged that I was hurting. "This is scary," I told myself. "You're afraid that he's going to get hurt and can visualize all this horrible stuff happening, like accidentally swerving out of the bike lane or an irresponsible driver. Right now, you feel pain, fear, and vulnerability."

Then, I acknowledged how many other parents feel the same way using that common humanity. "It's typical for parents to be concerned about their kids' safety. Many parents are. You're not alone in your fear."

The second part of common humanity is acknowledging the circumstances that have brought you this far, so I told myself, "You never experienced biking on streets like these as a kid. It's normal to feel scared of something that you don't have experience with."

Finally, I soothed myself. At that moment, I was on a bike right along traffic so this wasn't the time to cuddle up in a soft blanket or stay on the couch. I took a few deep breaths while riding and ran my fingertips gently down my arm a few times (as much as I could manage) so that I could calm my nervous system.

Did this completely take away my fears? No. But it did help me bring them under control enough so that I could remain present and not react strongly when my son inevitably swerved toward the edge of the lane before correcting himself again. I could calmly direct him to stay closer to the curb instead of, "OH MY GOD! BE CAREFUL! THESE DRIVERS CAN BE INSANE!" which would betray my fears and stress level.

TAKE ACTION

Next time you feel your self-critical Bob stepping in, ease yourself into the steps of self-compassion:

1. Recognize you're in pain. Your fear is causing an uncomfortable physical reaction in your body.

2. Remind yourself that you're not alone and others have felt similar fears.

3. Soothe yourself through an action that brings you comfort.

You don't have to criticize yourself to be better. Self-compassion brings comfort, understanding, and the strength to move forward.

Now, instead of resisting—which never works because that quarterback is way too powerful—you can practice these steps of self-compassion and give your benchwarmer a little more time to play and get stronger.

Next, we're diving into a topic your Bob excels at protecting you from and punishing you with in equal measure: embarrassment.

CHAPTER 8

"Everyone Thinks I'm Dumb."

The absolute hardest part of communication is figuring out what the other person is thinking. Many people often assume the worst and then act accordingly. Let's take a look at the steps to prevent assumptions and give yourself the permission to have better communication with your kids, partner, and people around you.

My husband and I walked into the back room of a pizza shop in Tucson—a place that, oddly enough, used to be a funeral parlor. That detail alone set an eerie tone, but what really had my heart in my throat was why we were there: my first high school reunion.

I prepared myself to see people that I hadn't seen in twenty years. None of the friends I still kept in contact with would be there. It was me on my own with my husband by my side. Would anyone even remember me? Would they want to talk to me? How awkward was this going to be?

High school wasn't difficult for me, but I wasn't necessarily popular. I stayed with my close group of friends, was on the swim team, and participated in a ton of extracurriculars. But underneath it all, I always thought I was lacking. Around the people I wasn't close to, my nerves spiked. I wanted to impress them. I wanted them to like me. And no matter how hard I tried, it never quite worked.

In my perfect world, I'd be welcomed everywhere—effortlessly connected, friends with everyone. But the reality stung. When I wasn't invited into certain groups, I told myself it was because I wasn't *enough*.

Not thin enough.

Not cool enough.

Not funny enough.

Not smart enough.

Going into this reunion was incredibly intimidating. I had grown personally since high school, having had two kids and publishing a book. It didn't matter how far I'd come, I still felt like the girl waiting to be invited to the table.

I prepared to try to prove myself again. I walked in and joined the first group in which I recognized a face, while my husband went to the bar to grab us both drinks.

While we chatted, I focused all my attention on my old German classmate. What's new with her? What's up with her? Classic tactic: take the attention off me.

As the evening rolled on, I talked with more people. What I found was that many of my old classmates who I thought hadn't noticed me or wouldn't remember me, were actually following me on social media. That whole fear of being hated, annoying or awkward, and never knowing what to say was universal amongst almost every one. Even those who I thought were so much smarter than me (the senior class president, for example) were more similar to me than I previously thought.

Did I change that much, or did I completely misattribute everyone's intentions?

Maybe the truth was simpler: I had always belonged—I just didn't know it.

If, right now, you have people in your life who you feel dislike or don't include you, you may be mistaken just like I was. When you're able to recognize this, a whole community opens up to you. Let's dig into how to do this.

THE THREE CONVERSATIONS

In the book *Difficult Conversations*, authors Bruce Patton, Douglas Stone, and Sheila Heen share the three different conversations actually taking place in every exchange that happens.[13]

The first conversation is the one in your head. It's what you think and feel. This can be your judgements about a situation, your feelings about an event, or what you want to say.

The second conversation is what the other person in the conversation is feeling. This is the dangerous one because we never know exactly

---

13 Douglas Stone, Bruce Patton, and Sheila Heen, *Difficult Conversations: How to Discuss What Matters Most*, 10th-Anniversary Edition (Penguin Books, 2010)

what the second conversation is, but we *think* we do. We think we know what people intend and why they didn't speak to us in high school, but we truly have no idea and no way to tell unless we ask them. Even then, we still may not get the correct answer.

The second conversation is where we struggle. Because we assume things that aren't true, accuse the other person of feeling or thinking those things, and then the entire conversation either turns into a screaming match or you get so flustered that you don't even attempt the conversation in the first place.

The third conversation is what an outside observer would see and agree with both of you happened. For instance, if you walk into your living room and see toys on the floor and a dish with little pieces of mac and cheese drying on it, a third conversation could go:

You, to your partner: "There are toys on the floor and a dirty dish on the table."

Outside observer (looking for facts): "Yes, this is true."

But that's not what happens in our everyday disagreements. Usually, when talking to someone we fall right into that tricky second conversation, assuming we know what the other is thinking and feeling and placing the blame on them. It may sound like:

You: "You never see it when the kids leave a mess around the house and always expect me to clean it up."

Outside observer, sticking to clear facts: "Whoa, hold up there. I can't confirm all that."

This mistake isn't just relegated to married life, but also happens in situations like high school reunions. I walked in anxious because I assumed what everyone thought of me. When I started to actually talk to others, I realized that I was wrong. Most of the time, the loudest voice judging us is our own.

WHEN WE STRUGGLE

We struggle with giving ourselves permission to do things when we get stuck in this second conversation. It causes us anxiety when we try to predict what others are thinking and assume the worst.

This isn't our fault. The human brain has a natural negativity bias and will always jump to such conclusions because evolutionarily it's kept us safe. Our life expectancy increased if we kept aware that a tiger might be hiding behind the next bush.

Today, the risk of tiger attacks is very low. That anxiety no longer serves us. Think of what happens when you assume the worst. For instance, email. Email can be so misconstrued—which is probably why my email messages are littered with happy emojis whenever I think I may come across even remotely harsh. I know that the smiley face conveys that I mean everything in a friendly way so that my requests don't become mischaracterized.

Perhaps you are someone triggered by emails. You read every piece of tricky news and information as if the deliverer is someone who doesn't like you or is looking down on you in some way. Obviously these people's emails are not littered with multiple smiley faces.

When your friend reads the same email, they don't see the threat that you feel is so obviously there. You're stuck in the second conversation, just like I was at my high school reunion. While it can be scary to jump out of the second conversation, it's essential. Not just for your own anxiety, but also for how people perceive and react to you. Your reaction to a perceived threat will project onto your next interaction with the person, possibly exacerbating an issue that wasn't there to begin with.

MY FIRST TONY ROBBINS EXPERIENCE

Tony Robbins is a world-renowned life coach who rose to fame in the early 2000s through transformational seminars, celebrity coaching, and his friendship with Oprah Winfrey. When I heard he was keynoting a conference I had tickets to, I was excited—and had no idea what to expect.

Let me say this: Tony Robbins is an experience. I was never more physically active watching a keynote than those four hours (yes, I said FOUR hours) that Tony was on stage.

Except he wasn't really on stage, he was walking through the audience, leading activities, getting people to move and jump up and down. I was in the aisle of a row in front and he walked by me twice. The man is massive. Every time he claps it's like watching two baseball catcher mitts coming together. I don't mean this as an insult, but rather to explain how Tony Robbins truly is a larger-than-life presence.

So when he asks you to do an activity where you're hugging random people, you do what Tony Robbins says.

"First," Tony instructed, "approach people like you are running late and you have somewhere else to be."[14]

We did that, scurrying from our seats and meeting five new people while acting like we have no interest in the conversation. Lots of folks smiled awkwardly and half-assed it, but me? I was game. Yes, Tony Robbins. Whatever you say, Tony Robbins.

Then, Tony progressed us through four additional scenarios, raising our energy levels as we moved from one to the next: late-for-a-meeting, high school acquaintance, friend you hadn't seen in twenty years, and finally your favorite person that you haven't seen in forever.

These last conversations were the most energetic, and even though logically I knew it was all pretend, they made me feel genuinely good. More energized. Happier. The point being that we have control over the energy we bring to a conversation. If we get stuck in the second conversation, our energy will be low and guarded. But if we can acknowledge that we have no idea what the other person is feeling and instead bring that energy of our whole, excited selves, our relationships can change in ways we never thought possible.

WHEN ARE YOU USING THE SECOND CONVERSATION?

How often do you think you know someone else's intentions? Through being a parent coach, I see it happen in the home with chores. Namely, when women assume their partner's and family's intentions around household tasks. Moms take on a large amount of the mental load when it comes to managing the home, everything from restocking toothpaste and toilet paper, to coordinating kids' appointments and

14 Tony Robbins, keynote address at Funnel Hacking Live, Las Vegas, NV, February 15, 2025.

feeding the dog, to reminding everyone to put away their things (kids and husbands included).

I know that is a broad generalization and need to admit right now that I am actually the one who leaves their stuff all around the house. It is my husband who is stifling his urge to tell me to put away the various pieces of mail I open and leave right where I opened them. I can speak from a place of deep understanding on this issue.

Many of my clients see the mess and assume that their family expects them to deal with it. They rely on Mom to keep the house clean. This is an example of using the second conversation. We assume intention ("they think I should clean it up") without evidence, and it builds resentment. Unless your family has told you explicitly, "Mom, we expect you to put this away," then it's probably not true.

For me, I typically get distracted and put my book down on a counter or take my shoes off in the middle of the hallway, meaning to come back and get them, and then I forget where they are. It's equally frustrating for me not being able to find where I left my stuff as it is for my husband to randomly come across it.

TAKE ACTION

Think of a situation in your life right now where you may be assuming the worst. Instead of making assumptions, focus on the facts of whatever is going on.

Use the third conversation to describe what you see and hear, and notice how the discussion changes.

PERMISSION SLIP

Give yourself permission to get curious about other people's intentions instead of assuming the worst.

In the next chapter, we'll dig into how to ask questions to find out others' true intentions in a way that works for parenting, as well as your adult relationships.

CHAPTER 9

"My Kids Are Doing This to Annoy Me."

Who hasn't seen a mess made by their kids made and immediately thought, *"They're doing this to make my life miserable!"*? Especially when you're tired and you can't process one more problem that you're responsible for solving. In this chapter, I'll show you how to approach this so that the problem is no longer yours alone.

PASTE ON THE LAWN CHAIRS

Lisa walked into her backyard to find her blue Adirondack chairs dripping with a thick, pasty white substance. Her two daughters, ages seven and nine, stood by painting the lawn furniture. Curious what they used?

They were very creative actually. They found that if you mixed flour and water together, you could paint with it. Yes, the girls had unknowingly stumbled on the recipe for papier mache, which as we know from many grade school art projects, dries as hard as a rock within a few hours.

Normally, Lisa would have lost her temper. However, she was one of my students in my parenting class, and in our last lesson we had just discussed the dangers of jumping to conclusions—that second conversation where we assume the worst.

First, Lisa calmed her own reaction. Normally, she would have yelled at her girls which would have then initiated their crying and she would be left in the backyard alone scrubbing papier mache off lawn furniture.

Instead, she used a framework that I refer to as HAPPY.

PARENTING BECAME EASIER

Eight years ago, I was sitting in a dental chair, mouth wide open, as the hygienist vented about her kids. She knew I was an elementary school teacher, so we were chatting about student behavior when she recommended a book that changed everything.

The book? *The Explosive Child* by Dr. Ross W Greene.[15] His whole approach centers around listening to kids instead of teaching through consequences and punishment. Up until then, all of my classroom management centered around positive discipline, which is letting kids make choices and giving them control. However, one of the drawbacks of positive discipline was that it left the teacher (me) or parent to infer the cause of the problem, something that's incredibly hard to get right.

15 Ross W. Greene, *The Explosive Child: A New Approach for Understanding and Parenting Easily Frustrated, Chronically Inflexible Children*, 6th ed. (Harper Paperbacks, 2021)

Dr. Greene starts with the assertion that "every child wants to do the best they can." Assuming malintent on the part of the kid is counter to this. He flips the parent/child dynamic from the parent knowing best in every situation, to the parent and child working together—both sharing their own intentions and needs—and then coming together on a solution.

As soon as I started using this with my own kids, my connections with them deepened dramatically. Parenting became easier because I was no longer guessing at what they needed and what they were trying to do. They were telling me. I had to refine a few of my questioning skills and monitor my own patience to master it, but the changes I saw in my mood and the greater ease I felt at home were life changing.

Being the teacher I am, I had to share it. I simplified a few parts and added a step that I found beneficial in my own practice. I turned it into an acronym to make it easy to remember.

THE HAPPY FRAMEWORK

HAPPY stands for:

H: Have Priorities

A: Appreciate Your Kid's Point of View

P: Process Your Own Emotions

P: Problem Solve Together

Y: Yield the Work

Let me take you through each, step-by-step.

Have Priorities

Kids cause chaos. It's true. They're little creatures with sticky hands running around with half-developed frontal lobes—they don't make the smartest decisions all the time. They're impulsive, easily distracted (I can relate), and constantly need reminders for basic tasks like "you need to eat" or "clean up your Legos before starting the next game." But they're also joyous, kind, and innocent. That's not to say you don't wish they'd cause a little less chaos, especially when you're trying to juggle adult responsibilities.

This first step, Have Priorities, encourages you to pick the most important issue you want to focus on and try to leave the rest.

Love and Logic, another parenting philosophy, encourages parents to stop fighting for control over everything, so they can influence what really matters[16]. This means giving up the need to have your kid's bedroom spotless, everything picked up from the living room, all the sibling arguments ceased, and grateful children that eat everything served for dinner without complaint.

What you get in return for giving those up is the power to influence your child when it comes to life choices—things that put them in danger—and their help and support when you really need it. This doesn't mean that you give up everything you want to happen in your house, nor that your child becomes a lazy slob. What it means is that you have to make the tough choice to focus on just one thing at a time if you want this to work.

---

16 Foster Cline and Jim Fay, *Parenting with Love and Logic: Teaching Children Responsibility* (Colorado Springs, CO: NavPress Publishing Group, 2020)

Ask yourself: What, if it were fixed, would make the biggest impact right now in our daily life?

If it is your child completing their chore list so that you have clean dishes for dinner each night, concentrate on that one. Work on the habit with them. Maybe you have been concentrating on one task and you don't see improvement. The next few steps of HAPPY will help you diagnose the problem and solve it *with* your child so you get results.

Appreciate Your Kids' Point of View

Was there a chore you hated as a kid that your parents needed to nag you to do? For me, it was the dishes. Ugh, I had to do those every night and HATED it (we didn't have a dishwasher, so it was me washing our family of four's dishes by hand).

Every night, I would try to wait out my dad to see if I could get into bed or watch so much TV before having to do the dishes. Every night, he kept on top of it and wouldn't let me "forget." Looking back, I had no choice in doing the dishes—it was assigned to me with no possibility of parole.

I hated putting my hands in the water, and finding room to fit every dish into the drying rack. Plus, every night, my dad still found a dish I would have to redo. This wasn't about apathy towards properly cleaned dishes, it was about not feeling seen. That's how chores were for a lot of us. They were assigned without discussion and our parents kept on us until we did it.

Looking back, this process took a huge amount of time and effort on the part of our parents. If you're hard on yourself that your kids don't do chores because you're "lazy," you're "inconsistent," and you just can't "follow-through," please hear me when I say this is not your fault. Expectations on parents and the distractions available have only increased in recent decades. In the eighties and nineties, it was more important that kids behaved and followed rules; now we have the benefit of time to show us the impact that those tactics have on mental health, as well as our relationships with our caregivers.

Millennial parents place a greater emphasis on more open communication and emotional intelligence.[17] When your kids fight you on chores, you know something doesn't feel right. Your kids become upset. They yell, they cry, and you can't rationalize that you're doing this "for their own good." Here's the gamechanger: **Your kids are fighting back because no one asked them their point of view.**

When it came to my disdain for dishes, there were specific things I hated about the act of dishwashing: the feel of water, the logic puzzle of the drying rack, and the loneliness of being in the kitchen by myself—all problems that we could have found solutions for. I would have stopped fighting. I would have felt cared for, rather than just brushed off with a "It's your job, do it." But digging deeper like this wasn't a common parenting practice in the eighties and nineties.

Thankfully, you have time on your side now. Start with my favorite question popularized by Dr. Ross Greene: "Hey, I notice you're [having difficulty with X] . What's up?"

---

17 "Raising Kids Now: Millennial Parenting Styles," *Parenting* blog, Ann & Robert H. Lurie Children's Hospital of Chicago, accessed August 10, 2025, *Parenting* blog, https://www.luriechildrens.org/en/blog/millennial-parenting-statistics/.

For example,

- "Hey, I notice you're having a challenge doing dishes at night. What's up?"

  or

- "Hey, I notice you're having difficulty getting ready for school on time. What's up?"

If your kids are like many of the kids of our Balance members, they will likely say, "Nothing," or "It's fine." That's because this is new. They're not accustomed to you wanting to know how they feel about it and so they're holding back. That's your cue to dig in deeper. You may even say, "I know in the past I haven't asked before. I'm not going to give you advice or tell you just to do it. I really want to know what's going on."

Your goal during the appreciate phase of HAPPY is to be a detective. Your job is to listen, not solve. Find out as much about the situation as you can without offering your opinion. The quickest way to shut your child down is interrupting this process with:

"Well, have you tried..."

"Oh, you should just..."

"That's silly, you shouldn't be worried about that."

Those statements are dismissive of your child's point of view and they will clam up so fast that you won't be able to hear their point of view.

I have a list of questions you can ask as follow-up and examples of conversations to use in the companion for this book at:

https:// noguiltmom.com/bestmom

Once you've listened to everything that your child has said, you're going to summarize for them. For me and the dishes it could sound like, "So you don't like putting your hands in dishwater, you're stressed out about trying to fit all the dishes in the drying rack, and you don't like being in the kitchen alone. Is there anything else?"

That "anything else?" is paramount. It's your confirmation to make sure you got all of the information. Once your child says, "That's it," you can move on to the next step. This is when your child feels seen—and that's the foundation for real collaboration.

Process Your Own Emotions

A common first reaction to this new way of parenting and communication is thinking that your opinions don't matter and your child now runs the house. This is far from true. What you're doing here is teaching the biggest negotiation lesson you will ever give your kids.

Negotiation doesn't mean winning. It's about reaching an agreement both sides can live with. This step is fairly short though. Remember how kids don't have a fully developed frontal lobe? If you offload all your very valid emotions of "not feeling appreciated," "feeling like you have to do everything around the house," and "never getting help," your kids simply aren't equipped to process and solve those.

This doesn't mean your emotions don't matter—they absolutely do. Those feelings need to be expressed and are best received among other parents who have experienced the same, know where you're coming from, and can help you through it.

When you process your emotions in a conversation with your kids about a problem, only two things matter:

1. How your kid's behavior affects them.

2. How your kid's behavior affects other people.

These two concerns are going to move the conversation forward. Here's what they might sound like in real life. Let's start with the dishes. How does not doing the dishes affect them? It could be something as simple as, "I know that dishes are boring, but they're a task that's necessary to keep you healthy so that you have clean surfaces to eat off of. I'm concerned that if you don't learn how to do them now, you won't know how to when you're an adult."

Or you can state how not doing the dishes affects others. For example, "We need clean dishes to eat from and cook with. When the dishes aren't done, it takes me longer to make dinner because I have to hunt the dish down and wash it before I can continue cooking. It's really frustrating." There's no single "right" response—just the one that feels most honest and constructive for you.

This phase is clearly stating a specific problem to be solved. Now with your problem explained and your kids' problem clearly defined, you can move on to the next step.

Problem-Solve

As a child, how many times were you told the solution to your problem and were then expected to do it? It might have sounded like, "Oh, that's easy. You should just…"

There it is. Problem solved and the adult walked away while you're left there with all the reasons why that solution won't work, but may have been told not to talk back so you kept silent.

Or maybe you did let it out, argue, and got punished for that. Many of us never learned how to problem-solve with others—especially not with adults. That's okay. You'll get better with practice. Just remember: This stage isn't about you fixing the problem. It's about your child leading the process, with your support.

That said, I want you to keep in mind a phrase that we use a lot in child development: Make this process child-led. Child-led means that your child is coming up with the ideas and you're there to assist as needed. Start the problem-solving stage by summarizing their point of view and your concerns. For example, the dishes problem-solving stage might sound like:

> "So I'm hearing you don't like putting your hands in the water, you feel stressed about the drying rack, and you don't like being in the kitchen alone while you wash the dishes. I'm concerned about not having clean dishes to cook with because the cooking time takes longer."

And then, the question: "I wonder how we can solve this?"

To which your child may look at you and say, "I don't know." This is normal! You are not doing anything wrong, nor are you stuck. You simply need to dig in with your questions to provoke curiosity and conversation. For example, you can ask:

- "Is there anything you would like to change about how you do dishes?"

- "Can we think of anything that might protect your hands?"

- "Do we need a bigger drying rack?"

- "What would make washing dishes easier?"

- "What would solve my issue of not having clean dishes for dinner?"

Since I remember this problem so distinctly after having this same fight for six years in childhood, I know exactly how I would have solved the problem:

1. I don't do the dishes anymore.

2. We buy paper plates and plasticware. Bam. No dishes.

3. You buy a damn dishwasher.

By the way, my parents did buy a dishwasher after I moved out. Am I still bitter? Yes, I hold a grudge. But now, I can laugh about it—and use it to help my own kids brainstorm better options.

Regardless, these solutions didn't work for my parents for a variety of reasons. If your kids give you solutions you don't agree with, that's okay! The point here is to find what Dr. Greene calls a "mutually-agreeable solution." So if one of those solutions comes up, you can say, "That doesn't work for me, let's keep thinking."

I ran into this same problem with my kids. We have a dishwasher, but the issue came with loading and unloading it. My teenage daughter was able to get into a rhythm with unloading, but my son avoided the task. Hard. Then, when he was reminded to do it, he'd get mad, stomping and crying.

I get it. I feel all the emotions just as deeply as he does. I get angry when someone tells me what to do, even when I tell myself what to do. There are two solutions I suggested that help me when I don't want to do a task.

One thing that helps is music. When I listen to something, it calms an angry part of my brain. For instance, I'm writing this book in my 6:00 a.m. writing session, which I am irritated about waking up for every single morning. I have a YouTube video playing in the background called "Study music & concentration" that's all soothing sounds, waves crashing on a beach, and spa music. It helps me calm down. My son found out that music helps him too, so we got him a pair of headphones and he blasts Eminem or AJR when unloading.

Another thing that helps is a timer. If I have a set amount of time I need to do the task, I can concentrate for that time. The abstract concept of completing unloading the dishwasher seems undoable, but unloading dishes for just ten minutes, *that* he can handle. So he sets his timer and unloads. Typically, he gets done in five.

Use your experience when suggesting options to your kids. It's of course up to them to try them, but I've found from working with parents, typically one of the parents deeply understands the inner workings of the kids' mind because it matches their own personality.

> This problem-solving causes many parents difficulty. If you want more examples, I've included them in the bonus for this book which you can find at: **https:// noguiltmom.com/bestmom**

Yield the Work

Yielding the work is the best part of the HAPPY process because this is when you step back and see how your child implements the agreed upon solution. I love this part because I enjoy seeing how people work, especially my kids, and I find it so interesting when stumbles happen that I didn't anticipate. Many people hate this part for the exact same reasons.

Yielding the work is unpredictable and you have no control of it. At first, you might see your child mess up and think, "This is never going to work! We need to go back to the other way!" That's fear talking—not truth.

You're going to want to step in and do it "right," and you'll wind up exhausted, resentful, and still doing it all this same time next year.

In her book, *Duct Tape Parenting*, parenting educator Vicki Hoefle suggests that parents need to stay out of the conflict and imagine that their mouths are sealed with duct tape.[18] Even better, they're tied to a chair with duct tape and can't jump up to help.

Kids develop confidence when they're allowed to struggle with issues and come to solutions on their own. That said, it's not like we should

18 Vicki Hoefle, *Duct Tape Parenting: A Less Is More Approach to Raising Respectful, Responsible, and Resilient Kids* (New York: Bibliomotion, 2012)

leave kids alone in this struggle. If they have ideas they need support on (such as me needing to buy my son headphones), support them. Have conversations with them about things that worked for you. But once they decide on a solution they want to try, **step back and let them do it.**

During this process, you will want the support of others as you see it through, because it's new and that path to the mailbox hasn't be packed down yet. Find a trusted friend that's reading this book too and support each other. Or consider joining our Balance community where every single woman is going through these same steps and has experienced the setbacks, struggles, and emotions that you'll feel throughout this process.

TAKE ACTION

Think of a behavior of your kid's that's irritating you. Perhaps you're always late leaving the house because they can't find their shoes. Maybe it's refusing to turn off screens and go to bed. In a moment when you're both calm, start with this now familiar question:

"Hey, I notice you're [having difficulty with X]. What's up?"

Then, ask further questions to get to the reason behind the behavior.

When you get curious about why your kid is acting the way they are and resisting you, you're going to find that 95 percent of the time, it's not about you at all. Of course, there may be behavior of yours that you want to change and I encourage that—afterall, controlling your own behavior is the only control you truly have. When you work through a problem using the HAPPY framework, you'll find issues lurking under the surface that have sensible solutions.

PERMISSION SLIP

This is your permission slip to get curious about the reasons behind your kids' behavior.

Once you're armed with this new information, you'll find it easier to take the next step that may seem hard for you right now: setting a boundary and sticking to it.

CHAPTER 10

"Everyone Gets Mad at Me When I Set a Boundary."

Boundary pushers. You probably have them in your life. People whom you tell no, and then they push back. Kids are natural boundary pushers. It's their job. Because of their pushback, you may question your boundary, maybe even calling yourself unreasonable and inflexible. Let's explore a simple strategy to state your boundary as plainly as possible to prevent boundary pushers from breaking through.

MY BARKING DOG DISTURBS THE NEIGHBORHOOD PEACE

"Is your dog okay?"

The text came in from my neighbor across the street as I sat working at my desk. I had recently moved into the neighborhood and this neighbor had come over and introduced himself. He seemed like a nice guy.

I immediately felt shame about my dog. You see, we affectionately call her a psychopath. She's a rescue we adopted at nine months of age from a local organization. Originally, she had been purchased as a puppy by a young couple, but then they had a baby and couldn't handle both so they gave the dog to a neighbor. The neighbor was the problem. We don't know the details, but whatever happened there left her traumatized.

As a result, my dog came along with huge anxiety and lots of barking. When we first moved, she would stand at the back gate looking out at the street and just bark and bark at every thing that walked by. My neighbor got the brunt of her barking.

I stared at the text confused, "'*Is my dog okay?*' Does he think I'm a horrible dog owner that doesn't take care of her pets?"

"Yes," I replied, "Sorry, she's a little crazy. I'll bring her in now."

All done, right? Wrong.

It happened again a few weeks later, "Is your dog okay?"

And then again, "Is your dog okay?"

Sigh, this time I was an hour and a half away at a cub scout event and was so tired of explaining that "Yes, the dog is okay." So instead I typed out, "Yes, she's fine. She's been outside for the day because we're out of town, but I'll be back soon."

That's when he lost it. Keep in mind, I thought we were friendly. Every interaction we had was pleasant and smiling. I even talked to him about the dog in person and he said that he just loved animals and wanted to make sure she wasn't in any pain.

He texted back, "YOU'RE NOT GOING TO BE HOME FOR ANOTHER 2 HOURS. THE DOG IS BARKING AND YOU ARE RUINING THE PEACE OF THIS NEIGHBORHOOD."

Whoa. That's a big reaction.

I thought, "Oh my gosh, I've read this situation all wrong. I now have to find a way to control my dog's barking so that we can leave our house for more than an hour at a time. He must hate me."

Nice Girl Me panicked. Boundary Me was furious.

All the same, my heart was beating fast—my anxiety took hold and I couldn't think straight. I decided to not answer him and just get home as quickly as I could. And then I felt guilty about my decision because my son and husband wanted me to stay longer, but I was in no head space to actually enjoy my time.

So I rushed home, brought the dog in (who was of course totally fine), and seethed. I ruminated. I thought of so many good comebacks. I was totally preoccupied with shame about the dog and anger at my neighbor. It took me three full days before I could think clearly enough again about the situation to reply. And when I did, I used a framework called PSAT.

MAKING PEOPLE LESS DEFENSIVE

I did not want to make an enemy out of my neighbor. I knew that I needed to be upfront about the situation and crystal clear in why I was upset. Most importantly, I wanted a productive conversation where we worked to solve the problem.

But unlike the HAPPY method that I use with people I'm really close to, I had no desire to dig in that deeply with my neighbor. To be honest, I was still annoyed—and not in the mood for deep emotional unpacking. This needed to be short and sweet.

The book *Crucial Conversations* has a great framework for talking about conflict.[19] The first thing to consider is what kind of conversation you need to have about the conflict. For that, there is the acronym CPR:

- **C: Content.** Is this a problem that only happened once?

- **P: Pattern**. Or is this a pattern of behavior and actions that you need to address? For instance, perhaps your husband forgot to take the trash bins out to the curb. He says he had a hard night and was up late working. You think, "But you have a hard night every week and this is the third time you've done it." That's because your problem concerns the pattern, not the content. When you switch to a conversation about that, he'll become less defensive about that one instance and may reflect on the problems causing the pattern that need to be solved.

- **R: Relationship.** This is when the same problem has happened for so long, it's starting to affect the relationship. You're losing trust in the person because you can't count on them. For example, you feel ignored because they're constantly late and you sense they don't value your time.

There's an additional letter for CPR and it deals with the way the conversation happens: P for Process. For instance, if every time you try to address an issue the person becomes defensive and starts denying

19 Joseph Grenny, Kerry Patterson, Ron McMillan, Al Switzler, and Emily Gregory, *Crucial Conversations: Tools for Talking When Stakes Are High*, 3rd ed. (McGraw-Hill Education, 2021).

everything, that's a sign to step back from the actual problem and talk about *how* you're talking about the problem.

A conversation like that may go, "It seems like when I bring up this issue, you appear to get upset and deny everything I'm saying. This makes it hard to move forward and find a solution. Can we talk about that?"

In the case of my neighbor, for me the issue was bordering between a pattern and a relationship conversation. This was something that had happened multiple times and I had even addressed it directly with him. I didn't just want to talk about what happened with his outburst via text, but rather the entire behavioral pattern that made it difficult for me to have a neighborly relationship with him.

PSAT

PSAT stands for Proof, Story, Ask, and Test. It's the method you can use for now and evermore to word your problems in a way that promotes problem-solving and minimizes defensiveness.

- Proof stands for the facts of the situation.
- Story is the story you're telling yourself about the situation and your feelings about it.
- Ask is making a specific request of the other person.
- Test is trying it out and even negotiating a little on what that specific request ultimately is.

Proof

Back in Chapter 8, we talked about the third conversation, the facts of the situation. It's what an outside observer can confirm is true. For instance, if your issue is that your husband doesn't do the dishes like he promised, the third conversation would be:

"When I walk into the kitchen in the morning, the dishes are still in the sink."

As opposed to your internal second conversation, which might sound like:

"You just expect me to do the dishes!" (Guessing what's going on in your husband's mind.)

The Proof element of PSAT is that third conversation. With my neighbor's text, I had to weed through all my emotions (such as "you're a maniacal ass") and figure out the *proof.* With this PSAT, I thought it best to write through text, because even after five days I was quite peeved. Plus, based on our last conversation not working out, I wanted something in writing that I could refer back to and confirm I didn't misstate anything.

I sat down to type out the proof:

"Hey, this past weekend, I received your text asking if my dog is okay. When I responded yes but I couldn't bring her in at the moment, you told me the dog was a disturbance to the neighborhood."

That's it for the proof stage. I don't yet bring up any emotions, instead referencing the exact event I'm referring to. Now, I want to provide a little more context. As I said earlier in the chapter, this was a pattern of behavior that I wanted to address, and not just an isolated incident. But to show the significance of the pattern, I needed to bring my story and feelings into it.

Story

Your story is how you interpret a situation, and it's so important to share with the other person. In order to have thriving relationships, each person needs to know how the other reacts and responds to circumstances.

Your emotions and feelings are important. But here's where it gets tricky: navigating between the 2nd person and 1st person conversation in explaining emotions. When I was first getting the hang of this method, I found that a lot of the emotions I experienced were caused by my assumptions about the other person's intentions.

I was already defending myself when there was no defense needed. For example, in this situation it was easy for me to assume that he thought I was a cruel, irresponsible person with no regard for the people around me. Even writing that is hard for me, because I do think that's what he assumed. If someone was taking bets, I would be pretty confident putting all my money on that one.

But stating that assumption didn't belong in my conversation. Because on the off-chance that I was wrong, he would probably have taken offense and spent more of his energy defending himself than actually listening to my concern. I wanted my concern heard. It's a choice.

So, I continue in PSAT with my Story. With the story, I added in my feelings and interpretations, being careful to make sure I was talking only about myself and sticking in that first person conversation.

> "I want to explain how I felt so you know where I'm coming from.
> I was confused when I got your message, because when we talked
> a few weeks ago I asked you if my dog's barking was bothering you

and you said that no, you were just concerned that the dog was okay. I was also hurt by your comment that I was disturbing the peace of the neighborhood."

Yes, I said I was hurt. That's a hard phrase to write and put out there. I would have felt much safer telling him how deplorable his actions were and how he needed to be more respectful. But, you know how that would go. Nothing solved.

Notice how in the story, I reference what was said, but I made the feelings my responsibility. Now, I needed to figure out what I wanted. But I didn't know what I wanted yet. I couldn't ask without more information about exactly where he was coming from. So I left my text as it was and pressed Send. I waited for a response.

I know that people need thinking time in a situation like this. It's a hard thing to hear how your behavior affects another person, so I never like to deliver that news in person if I don't see them every day.

From experience, my heart will start pounding in my chest any time someone asks me to "talk." Oh my gosh, please never ask me to "talk." My brain is an anxious vortex and the situation will not go well.

Case in point, a friend once told me she felt icky when I stepped into a situation between her and her son. I reacted, "I'm just such a horrible person! And I'm sorry! I have to go!" I hung up the phone in tears.

I have big reactions mastered now, and I'm embarrassed by them. I know I really appreciate it when people give me a heads up on the issue and what they're thinking in a non-confrontational way so that I can feel my big emotions in private and be given a chance to cool down and come back to the conversation in a logical frame of mind.

Now, this doesn't mean I expect the same from other people. It's a courtesy I like to give others. When other people confront me, I'm doing my best now to use a cut-and-dried phrase of, "Thank you for bringing this to my attention. Let me process this and get back to you."

Then I walk away and scream all the expletives, cry, journal, and process the hell out of the emotion.

All this to say, I understand why my neighbor took four days to get back to me. He brought context to the situation too.

I saw the notification from him pop up on my screen and opened the text.

"I'm sorry. I've been told that I'm really direct and so I was trying to soften my approach by asking if your dog is okay."

With that single message, I totally understood how the miscommunication happened. He was dealing with his own emotions and trying the best he could. When the situation didn't resolve, he became understandably angry.

Got it. Now I had enough information to make my ask.

Ask

Ask is what you would like to see happen. When I'm texting, I often don't make a specific ask. In close relationships, like with my husband or friends, I might say something like, "How do you see it?" because I want their perspective before we find a solution. But sometimes, like with my neighbor, a clear ask isn't even necessary. Just being heard can be enough.

I don't want Ask to be a stumbling block for you. If you don't know exactly what you want from the situation, it's okay. This can be a sign that you need more information, or that you're hurt and all you want is the other person to acknowledge your feelings.

I need to give you a heads up with this whole process at this point. In our society, we have been told to hold everything in and not express our true emotions. It can be incredibly overwhelming to the other person to hear everything going on in your head. It's why I also like to include an apology of sorts when I'm sharing my proof and story, before I make my specific ask.

The apology is, "I'm sorry, I should have shared how I was feeling sooner. That's on me."

This applies to conflict that exists in our everyday life, like squabbles with neighbors, your partner not doing the housework—any situation where there is miscommunication and misunderstanding. In these situations, an apology is powerful. (Sidenote: This is *not* in the case of abuse, because if you're abused, it's absolutely and unequivocally not your responsibility. Your brain is traumatized by the situation and I recommend seeking the help of a professional to figure out what to do.)

Why? Because when you take responsibility for your contribution, the person you're in conflict with won't feel the need to defend themselves. Their guard will lower and you will find that instead of fighting tit-for-tat, you can come to a solution quicker. What I've found in most of these situations is that the other person will take responsibility for their contribution as well.

But perhaps you do this, and you find the other person takes *all* the responsibility. Not in a productive way, but in a, "I'm the most horrible person in the whole world and I'm to blame for everything" sort of way.

Hi! I'm JoAnn. And that's my first response to every problem brought to me.

I can speak from intense, painful experience on this one. I don't do it as a way to play and manipulate people's emotions (I've heard that one before and that accusation is extremely hurtful).

Some people yell and blame others when they get angry. I work with a lot of parents who tell me, "I can't stop myself from yelling and then I feel bad. How do I control it?"

Remember how we talked about those snowy paths to the mailbox, and how our neurons are wired together to act in habit? That's what happens when someone immediately resorts to yelling, and what happens when I immediately feel shame. It's unconscious and I'm just wired that way.

That doesn't make it an excuse. But if you find someone else has this reaction, it's not your fault and you don't have to try to fix it. When you're on the other side, let it be. As Mel Robbins suggests in her book, *The Let Them Theory: How to Stop Controlling Other People and Start Living Your Life*, go ahead and let them have those emotions.[20] Then, decide what you're going to do with yourself. You can simply say, "I see you may need some time to process this. I'm going to give you that space, and we can talk when you're ready." And then exit and wait. This keeps it firm yet compassionate.

20 Mel Robbins, *The Let Them Theory: How to Stop Controlling Other People and Start Living Your Life* (HarperCollins, 2024)

What's a reasonable ask? You don't need a fully baked solution or a perfect plan when you make your ask. Just an idea is enough to start.

With my neighbor, once I realized that he was trying to counter his tendency to be harsh and direct, I knew what to ask for. I replied, "Next time my dog barks, can you let me know and I'll bring her inside?" He agreed.

As another example of an ask, I was talking with one of my kids about "phubbing." If you haven't heard this term, it means phone snubbing, aka when you're sitting next to someone and instead of talking to you, they ignore you and pay attention to their phone. In this case, my ask was not to be ignored in public. Especially since it was just the two of us and I had no one else to talk to.

When I made this ask, my child explained how they got overwhelmed and didn't feel like talking at times.

I get that, and I can also find my own entertainment when I'm told that's the case. With this ask, I needed more information about how my child felt. We didn't come to an agreement, but both of us now have knowledge of what the other is going through and we can move to Test.

Test

Once you've shared your proof, story, and made your ask, it's time to move into the final phase: test.

The test phase takes an undetermined amount of time. Depending on the circumstances, it can last days or months. You're waiting to see, when the situation arises again, what happens? Are things different?

Did the other person change their behavior? Did you change your behavior?

Test doesn't mean that now the relationship is perfect and all the problems are solved. In the case of my neighbor, we didn't talk much after and I definitely put up somewhat of a wall between us. He had blown up at me over text and I kept my distance because I didn't want that reaction again. I was hurt, I was scared, and that takes time to heal.

I was also very proud that I didn't just hide from the situation—I confronted it head on. He waved "hi" when he walked his dogs and I waved back. He had these issues with other neighbors as well, and my hunch is that he wasn't self-aware enough yet to realize what was going on in his brain and causing these issues. He was getting there. When he apologized to me, he acknowledged how he tended to be harsh. My suspicion is that he didn't understand social cues. I noticed this in my interactions with him, which felt uncomfortable and jilted. I assumed that he was neurodiverse and gave him a lot of grace.

My other neighbor did not understand that and got into long drawn-out fights with him. They would yell at each other and then she'd bemoan what an awful neighbor he was. He ended up moving away six months later. They never resolved their conflict and caused stress for each other in the meantime. It's an example of what happens when you assume and don't ask questions.

Do you have an issue right now that you've been avoiding bringing up? Put your concerns in the PSAT format.

- **Proof:** Find the facts of what happened. Beware of any assumptions of what the other person is thinking, or their intentions. Those can be invasive.

- **Story:** Share your own feelings and what you're telling yourself about what happened.

- **Ask:** Make your ask for what you want to happen. Know that you may need to modify your ask based on what the other person has to say.

- **Test:** Agree to a solution and see how it works.

PERMISSION SLIP

This is your permission to set a boundary even when—especially when—you expect a huge emotional reaction from the other person. You can also ignore the age-old advice of having these conversations in person, since text or email may help you stay objective and non-reactive when confronted with the other person's emotions.

Now that you know how to discuss a boundary, let's dig a little deeper into how you spend your time.

CHAPTER 11

"I Know What My Kids Want, But What About Me?"

Right now, I bet you're selflessly devoting large chunks of your time to your kids. We're programmed this way as moms to protect our young. The problem arises when we spend so much time devoted to our children, that we forget what we want for ourselves.

The first time I met my friend Ruth was on a film set. What really impressed me was that it was a set of her own making. I had retired from my job as a teacher a few years prior and was pursuing my own business full time. At the time, that consisted mostly of blogging and selling my own products.

I saw an ad on Facebook for a course called Elite Blog Academy and thought, "Yes! I want an elite blog." So I signed up. Ruth taught me how to attract people to my site and how to structure my writing. A few months later, I signed up for her mastermind program, and one of the perks was being invited to Seattle to be a part of the re-filming of the course.

As I walked in and saw all the people milling around, the quiet conference room with just Ruth in front of a camera and a teleprompter, and all of these people coming together to create something—I wanted it. I wanted it badly. I didn't even know it was something that was possible until I walked into that hotel lobby. Sometimes you don't know what you want until you meet it face-to-face.

A year later, Ruth moved the mastermind to her office in Punta Gorda, Florida. Ten of us met in the front room of the house she had purchased downtown. Ruth's books and planners lined the bookshelves right by the entrance. She had her own filming studio set up in another room where she could create her own content with professional lighting. It felt big and important, and I wanted it.

At that mastermind meeting, we talked about our goals and our visions for our own companies. I wanted my own studio. I wanted to do in-person retreats. I wanted to be a *New York Times* bestselling author. These were all things that before I never even knew I wanted *because I didn't even know they were possible.*

REDEFINING ENVY

Most of us women have been taught that envy is bad. "Don't be envious, it's a sin," we were told. Elise Loehnen in her book, *On Our Best Behavior*, encourages women to reframe envy as a signal.[21] When it appears, it means that it's something you want.

---

21 Elise Loehnen, *On Our Best Behavior: The Seven Deadly Sins and the Price Women Pay to Be Good* (New York: Dial Press, 2023).

I've coached many women who, when they first start with me, don't know what they want. They've spent so long focused on their kids and families that they've lost touch with what actually lights them up. Envy can be a tool in this case. When I see Ruth with "*New York Times* Bestselling Author" next to her name, I'm envious. I want that title so bad. Yet, there's another voice (Bob) who tells me, "Sure, she did it, but it's impossible for you," or when he's feeling a bit more generous, "Yes, she did it, but it took hard work combined with luck." Who's to say that if I worked as hard as Ruth did that I would achieve the same thing?

Remember, Bob's sole job is to keep you safe. It's to keep you comfortable, to not push you out of your comfort zone so that you don't have to experience failure and regret. I see you, Bob, and I acknowledge you, but I'm still sitting down every day to write this book.

So why keep going when Bob tells me the odds are slim and the effort might not pay off? Because seeing the achievement is one thing, but witnessing the hard work—the mess, the fear, the tears—that's even more powerful.

I was in Ruth's mastermind when she was writing her second book, *Do it Scared*, and I had the privilege to see what a taxing process it is to write a book. Ruth was vulnerable about the emotions and fear going through her head as she wrote the book. I also got to see her take the TedX stage in Denver, Colorado, speaking to an audience of five thousand as a result of that book.

It wasn't seeing her success that drove me forward, it was seeing the struggle that led up to it. Because writing is a huge struggle. Every morning at 6:00 a.m., I go down to my basement office. Just getting there is hard. Convincing myself to peel out of bed and show up to my computer to put my 1,000 to 1,500 words down is a struggle.

I constantly criticize my work, telling myself I can't write. I don't know how to punctuate well. My grammar is awful. And yet I know that throughout the whole process, all these feelings are normal, because I saw someone else go through them.

YOU HAVE TO SEE IT TO BE IT

As moms, and I see this in women I coach, we feel guilty taking time for ourselves to work on our own ventures. It's scary when we take time that we could be spending on our kids, especially when there are no guarantees that our own things will work out. Wasting time is one of the biggest fears I hear from women in my community.

I hear women say things like:

- "I wasn't very productive."
- "My kids woke up and I didn't get much done."
- "I'm so tired and I don't want to sit down and do anything else."

This guilt is rooted in deeper systems—like the Protestant work ethic that's baked into American culture. It's the idea that productivity equals morality. That hard work is a virtue, and rest is laziness.

When you trace your thoughts back to their cultural origins, they start to lose some of their grip.

But here's the thing: We want our kids to achieve big things and be gloriously happy, but they have to see it to be it. My dad was a teacher and I knew exactly what that was like, what it entailed, the ups and downs. My mom was in hospital administration. I knew what an office job looked like. And it is no coincidence that before I started my online business, I was both in an office position and then I became a teacher. I went toward what I knew.

Your kids will do the exact same thing. To put it bluntly: If they see you self-sacrificing everything for your family (even if they say they will never do such a thing), it will be what they know and they will go toward that. The familiar is always easier than what's scary. That's why it's so important for you to go for that scary thing that you want. Go toward that envy. Pick it apart and see what it is that you actually want. In doing so, you're not only doing it for you, you're doing it for your kids.

As popularized by tennis phenom Billie Jean King, "you have to see it to be it."

TAKE ACTION

What are you feeling envious about right now? It may appear as, "I wish I had time for that," or, "I don't know how she does all that."

Use your envy as a signal that this may be something you want to do too. Explore that.

Give yourself permission to pursue that new thing that you want. Sign up for a class. Watch a YouTube video. Take one tiny action to explore what may light you up.

Up next, we're tackling the fear of that activity "taking too much time."

CHAPTER 12

"What If It Takes Too Long and Isn't Worth It?

You know that phrase people use when you say a task will take too long, *"Time will pass anyway"*? I want to tell you that accomplishing a goal is *not* the only benefit you'll get from going after something big. Finishing the task won't be your only reward, because other surprising benefits await you, too. Let me show you what I mean.

NATIONAL BOARD CERTIFICATION

I first heard about National Board Certification as a second year teacher. I had just gotten my Master of Education and, being the achiever I am, felt it was a way to challenge myself and get that validation I crave.

I convinced my friend Chelsea, who taught in the classroom beside me, to get National Board Certified as well. It is a long, cumbersome process. So much so, that both of us took a class dissecting the process, learning about the National Teaching Standards before we even officially committed to the process.

I like to tell people that my National Board Teaching Certification was way more work and effort than my Master's degree. To be certified, I needed to complete four portfolios where I analyzed my students' work and presented my case, like a lawyer, as to how I was an accomplished teacher. And it wasn't just the portfolios. I also had to sit for a three-hour exam that would test my knowledge of teaching all the subject areas as an elementary school teacher. I needed a score of 270 to pass.

It took me about four months to complete each portfolio, and then five months of waiting for my score. My friend Bridget from high school was also going through the process. Our mantra was "one and done." For the National Board, you have three years—three tries—to pass. If you didn't pass the first year, you could pick specific portfolios or sections of the test that you didn't do well on and just redo those without having to resubmit the entire thing.

One and done. One and done.

The morning of the score release, I logged onto the site. I got a 256, fourteen points below what was necessary. My friend Bridget passed on the first try.

Devastated. Defeated. I had never gone after something so big and daunting and failed.

That's the risk with big goals. You may fail. All that time may pass and you'll have nothing to show for it. But that's not entirely true.

HOW BIG ARE YOUR GOALS?

I was twenty-nine when I first attempted National Board Certification, and up until that point, I had never put myself in a position where I could truly fail. I didn't apply to any college I thought I couldn't get into. I never auditioned for anything in theater that felt too big for me. I played it safe.

The failure of the National Board Certification had me crying for days. Every time I thought about it, I would break down in tears. I didn't even know if I wanted to try again a second time. Redo all that work, all that effort, all that time. What if I didn't make it again?

Here's something I've learned about goals: If you're certain you can achieve them, they're probably not worth going after. A big statement, right? But here's why I believe it. A goal shouldn't just be something to check off a list. It should be a process that changes you. A challenge that rewrites a belief you hold about your potential. Something that, when you reach it, leaves you different than when you began.

I thought SMART goals were the way to go. If you're not familiar with SMART goals, they stand for:

- Specific: You must define your goal so that it's not too broad.

- Measurable: Be able to measure progress on it.

- Achievable: Make sure you can reasonably accomplish your goal in a certain time frame.

- Relevant: Make sure they are aligned with your long-term goals and values.

- Time Bound: They should be relegated to a certain time frame.

SMART goals have their place—week to week, day to day. But when it comes to something that will change you, you won't find it in a SMART goal. You'll find it in a DREAM goal.

WHAT'S A DREAM GOAL?

DREAM is an acronym I created to help women evaluate whether they're setting goals that will truly change them, or just goals they can check off a list. It's a list of five qualities that your goal should have: Daunting, Research Needed, Emotions, Audacious, and Mentally Visible.

Is it Daunting?

When I started the National Board Certification process, I was scared. It felt like it would take way too long and pile on stress I frankly didn't need. I was a full-time teacher with a two-year-old at home—pursuing something this big seemed a little nuts. And yet, I knew it was necessary.

I've learned through time that if my goal didn't make me feel just a little sick, it wasn't worth going after. Research supports this. Psychologists Edwin A. Locke and Gary P. Lantham first coined the term "stretch goals."[22] They found that pursuing a goal outside of your current skill set promotes the growth of new neural pathways, problem solving behaviors, and resilience.

Mihaly Csikszentmihalyi, the psychologist who coined "flow", found that people experience the highest levels of growth and satisfaction

---

22 Edwin A. Locke and Gary P. Latham, "New Directions in Goal-Setting Theory," *Current Directions in Psychological Science* 15, no. 5 (2006): 265–68.

when a goal slightly exceeds their skill level.[23] Additionally, people are more likely to stay stimulated and not get bored.

When you think about your goals, do they make you feel a little queasy? Queasy like, "Oh my gosh, this is HUGE. I can't believe I'm even attempting this. I can't do this."

That's the feeling you want when going after a goal. I always look for, "I can't do this." Because if I thought I *could* do it, it wouldn't be worth going after.

Research Needed: Do you know how to achieve it?

I'll be honest, National Board Certification confused me. There were so many standards that I had to meet, but no examples of how to meet those standards because the board wanted to see your unique thinking. When I didn't achieve certification the first time, I thought the National Board was stupid. I thought that the reason I didn't achieve it was because it was vague, they were wrong, and the process was unfair.

I didn't know how to reach my goal. This is an indicator that I was pursuing something big enough. I needed to research and learn more to be able to achieve it.

Was all the emotion, anguish, and work from the past year really worth it? I was ready to quit. So, I sat in my feelings—bought a gorgeous pair of boots with them—then, a few weeks later, got on a call with one of my coaches, Alaina. Alaina said something that has stuck with me and guided me through every challenge since. "JoAnn, you are

23 Mihaly Csikszentmihalyi, *Flow: The Psychology of Optimal Experience* (New York: Harper & Row, 1990).

92 percent of the way there. You've made it SO far. Now, you need to concentrate on just that final 8 percent. You aren't starting over."

That one mindshift gave me the courage to start on my second year of National Board Certification and figure out how to achieve it. As luck would have it, my district had just invested in a new program that worked on kids' developmental writing skills in a systemized manner. In fact, what I learned from teaching that program, I still use in my own writing today.

I had to learn a new skill for teaching writing that I would never have learned if I had not failed the National Board Certification the first time. I gained a deeper understanding, and because of that, I increased my score on the writing portfolio by ten points!

Does it bring up strong emotions?

When I ask my coaching clients about their goals, 80 percent of them say decluttering the house. A research study from UCLA showed that the amount of the stress hormone cortisol in people increases when they are in a cluttered environment. We all know that reducing stress is worthwhile.[24] However, there is an issue if decluttering is your never-ending goal. You can get stuck. Does decluttering inspire you? Does it light your heart on fire? You may be using decluttering as a failsafe.

A DREAM goal needs to stir strong emotions—the kind that inspire you to keep showing up. But with that, it will also bring the hard stuff. When I failed the National Board Certification, I cried. I cried hard.

24 Darby E. Saxbe and Rena L. Repetti, "No Place Like Home: Home Tours Correlate with Daily Patterns of Mood and Cortisol," *Personality and Social Psychology Bulletin* 36, no. 1 (2010): 71–81

I cried long. I had to feel all the emotional lows and move through them before I was ready to try again.

Sadness, grief, and despair are emotions that we as humans try to avoid. The first time you let yourself feel those emotions, they can feel intensely overwhelming and you may think, "Why did I do this to myself?" and "Is this goal even worth this anguish?" But I'm telling you—it is. It's worth all of it. When you allow yourself to fully feel your emotions instead of avoiding them, they pass. You metabolize them. They give you strength and insight. You can then coach your kids through their disappointments, because you've been there. You've made it to the other side.

How powerful is that? Instead of just saying, "Don't quit," you can say, "I know it's hard. I've been there. And if you keep going, you'll find your way out."

If your current goal doesn't have the capacity to stir up all of this in you, it's not big enough. Aim higher because you are capable of so, so much.

Audacious: How do you feel telling other people your goal?

One thing I've learned about goals: When you share them with others, you may see their fear or doubt. Your goal should be audacious and not easily accomplished. If it's not audacious, you will not learn or grow as a person when you try to go after it.

When I told people I was going after National Board Certification, I got the same responses: "It's not worth it," and "What do you get from it? Nothing." Which is kind of true, if you look at it in terms of recognition and compensation. My school district offered nothing but a congratulations for getting National Board Certified. All that work, all that research, all the measurable improvement to my teaching, and all I would get is a pat on the back. How could that be worth it?

But it did bring with it a certain cache that made me feel good about achieving it. The amount of work made it seem like an audacious goal, as well as the fact that many people who tried it, didn't make it. It wasn't a guaranteed "do this work and you'll get certified," as I saw my first time through.

It was audacious. How can I think that I will be the one to accomplish this?

Same goes for starting a business, writing a book, and anything creative. There are no guarantees you'll succeed. Audacity and emotions go hand in hand. Some nights, I get so down about my ten-year-old business, that I consider what it would be like to quit and walk away. My business is my DREAM goal. There is no endpoint. I ride the waves of ups and downs.

I just had this experience last night as we've seen a shift in the online business industry, and I'm trying like mad to figure it out. Revenue is down and I'm having a hard time finding how to pick it up again. I went to bed so depressed by the realization that I'm going to have to borrow money to keep it afloat. Thankfully, this feeling is not new and I've been through so many of these dips before. I know that one idea, one change in strategy, can bring the whole business bouncing back.

This morning, as I sat down to write, I checked our business dashboard and found that two big sales came in overnight brought on by a new strategy. Suddenly, I'm hopeful again. That's what goals do. When you set one, you buckle your seat belt and ride the emotional roller coaster. Sometimes you're climbing a hill you fear will never end, and others you're coasting through sheer exhilaration.

Mentally Visible: Can you see it?

The last piece of a DREAM goal is that it needs to be mentally visible. Do you know what you're going after? Can you visually see it? If you tell me that you can mentally see your clean house, close this book and take a time out. Decluttering is not a DREAM goal.

I want you to be able to see the thing that you're about to create. There is so much power in visualizing. Olympic swimmer, Michael Phelps, described how before every race, he mentally rehearsed everything from starting on the starting blocks to diving in the water[25]. He envisioned how this stroke felt in the water and how he passed one of his competitors in the lane next to him.

Your goal needs to be so clear that you can see it. See yourself going through the motions—every step leading to success. When I was working on my National Board Certification, I could picture myself logging into the portal and seeing that I'd passed. I could see my name on the school marquee, congratulating me as a newly certified teacher.

Can you truly see yourself accomplishing your goal? What emotions does that stir inside you?

The second time I pursued National Board Certification, I could see achieving it so clearly.

---

25 Mackenzie Wagoner, "What We Can Learn from the Olympics: How to Train Your Brain Like a Champion," *Vogue*, August 23, 2016, https://www.vogue.com/article/how-to-train-your-brain-like-an-olympic-athlete-power-pose-mental-exercises-for-confidence

However, I fell one point short. One point! I thought surely they would give it to me for one point. I could request a rescore, something. But, no.

Thankfully, this time I didn't fall into such a deep despair over it. I knew that my test on teaching reading could have been higher. I signed up to retake one thirty minute test and read a book recommended to me on teaching reading and analyzing what a student needs to work on. I am so grateful for that book because it taught me, as a teacher, material that I didn't even know I needed.

The only drawback was that I wasn't a classroom teacher anymore when I retook the test. My son was born in July and I had decided to take a year off to stay home with him. When I received my scores the following October, I had already started my company, No Guilt Mom, and didn't get to use my certification in the classroom.

I never got my name on a marquee—and I'm okay with that. All those fears I had about it taking too long or it not being worth it? They were unfounded. It didn't turn out how I expected, but the benefits I ended up with were better than what I'd been chasing.

That National Board Certification process is a testament to my endurance. Whenever I find myself facing what feels like setback after setback, I look back on those three years of trying, waiting, failing, and having to start all over again. But eventually, I made it.

That's what I carry with me now. And that's what I want for you. You're going to struggle, but eventually, you're going to make it too.

TAKE ACTION

What is your DREAM goal? Name that achievement or experience you've always wanted that may scare you to go after. Make sure that it's:

- **D: Daunting.** Your goal should scare you.

- **R: Research Needed.** You don't know exactly how to achieve it now. You'll have to learn how.

- **E: Emotions.** You care deeply about the objective and it will take you on an emotional roller coaster. This is where massive growth happens.

- **A: Audacious.** That look of trepidation in family and friend's eyes tell you that you're pointed in the right direction. This goal is not for the person you are now, it's for the person you're going to be.

- **M: Mentally Visible**. You need to see yourself achieving it. What does it look like?

PERMISSION SLIP

Don't let time and "it'll take too long" stop you from trying. Your DREAM goal is going to change you as a person.

But if you're stuck in the mess of prioritizing everything that's on your to-do list right now, you may be nervous about attempting a DREAM goal. Let's get into how to separate your "should-do's" with your "want to-do's" in the next chapter.

CHAPTER 13

"I Know I *Should.*"

When you feel caught up in everything on your to-do list that you feel you "should" do, it can feel near impossible to make time for anything else. What may help is clarifying your values.

I'M NOT A DEAL SHOPPER

I absolutely hate shopping. My ideal life would include having someone make all the decisions for me, telling me what to buy, and I'd just do it. Especially when it comes to clothes. I feel this nagging guilt every time I find a piece of clothing I like and look at the price tag. And not even that large of a price tag, say $50 for a pair of pants that feel great and look absolutely gorgeous.

I think to myself, "Shouldn't I try to find something cheaper?" Yet my defiant spirit rebels. I don't want to go bargain shopping. I don't want to find anything cheaper. Damnit, why does this have to take so much time?

I was interviewing my friend, Rachel Nielson from the *3 in 30 Podcast*, about values and she confessed to me a gamechanger.[26] "Thift isn't one of my values," she admitted.

What?! We have a choice about whether thrift is a value? I thought thrifting was just something "good, responsible people" did—and that not caring about bargains made me a pariah. My jaw dropped. I realized I'd spent the past forty years suffering for nothing.

You may laugh and think this is a little intense, but this was a huge revelation for me. To think I could be unapologetically happy, living in a way that makes sense to me, without wasting time and energy on what I "should" do to be a good person. Perhaps you're living this same way.

I took Rachel's advice and did a value sort.

HOW TO DO A VALUE SORT

I created a tool to help you do this. It's available in the companion pack for this book at **https:// noguiltmom.com/bestmom**

First, you'll start with a list of a hundred values and go down the sheet marking: Definitely Yes, Maybe, or No. It's a first-impression kind of thing. Each value should land in a pile based on your gut—no overthinking allowed.

---

26 Rachel Nielson, interview by JoAnn Crohn, November 1, 2024, for the Happy Mom Summit.

When you complete the list, go back through your Maybes and make definite yes or no decisions on those.

You'll end up with a list of possibly ten or more yeses. Your job is to reduce that list into five or fewer. With some of mine, I combined values and made up my own value names. My final list of values is: community, growth, adventure, and creative contribution. Notice that thrift is nowhere. It's not allowed to come close to my list of values.

Why do this?

Figuring out my values helps me make decisions and also points me in new directions of what I want to try and pursue. As a mom, it's incredibly hard not to get wrapped up in what everyone else needs and not pursue anything new yourself. My values help guide my decisions and whether to say yes or no to opportunities or invitations.

For instance, I can be feeling down and not knowing why. When I look at my values, I find that I'm not honoring any of them. I've been holed up in my basement office, alone on my computer. No adventure. No other people. My values tell me: "Hey JoAnn, contact your friends and plan a girls night," or, "Start planning a trip somewhere new where you can have an adventure."

They also help me fully embrace decisions like buying yet another book because growth is one of my core values. I feel zero guilt because I'm living in alignment with what matters to me. When I hesitate about something, I run it through my values test.

Typically, my hesitation is for a reason related to wanting to please someone else or keep up with my own unwanted expectations of what I should be doing. For example, sometimes my desire for my kids to like me keeps me from standing up for myself. Since they're both teens—or close to it—I've been giving them more independence, especially around food. That's created a new challenge: dinner. Many nights, after I've cooked, both of them tell me they're not hungry because they've been snacking.

One of my values is connection, and dinner time is when we get that family connection. Part of me wants to roll with their decision and say okay, but knowing my value is connection alerts me to why I'm so troubled by this. As a compromise, even though they're not hungry, I ask that they come sit at the table with us all so we can be together and talk.

Naming your own values helps you solve complex situations. It's like a laser focus that guides you in how to proceed instead of getting stuck in indecision.

Terri, a mom in Canada and Balance member, remembers fighting with her son's school over the teachers' and administrators' perceptions of his behavior. Her son is on the autism spectrum, and the teachers wanted him to adjust some of his behaviors. Once Terri realized that one of her core values was uniqueness, it all clicked. She understood exactly why she was so upset: She never wanted to teach her kids to mask or conform just to fit in.

TAKE ACTION

I kept this chapter short to encourage you to take one, necessary action: Define your values. Once you know what's important to you, so many priorities in your life become clear.

I made a value sort tool to help you in the free companion to this book at **https:// noguiltmom.com/bestmom**

PERMISSION SLIP

You have permission to say no to the things that don't align with your values. When you do that, you'll find that prioritizing your to-do list becomes manageable.

Now, we need to dig into one more hurdle that may be overcrowding your to-do's: saying no to other people's problems, especially your kid's.

CHAPTER 14

"I Can't Set Boundaries."

Saying no to your child when you feel that you should be able to say yes is a hard roadblock for many women. However, sometimes setting your boundary and allowing for natural consequences is the best teacher of all.

THE PAIN OF NATURAL CONSEQUENCES

I was driving home from college down I-10, nearing the curve by Casa Grande, when my car made a loud, jarring sound like metal on metal. A few warning lights flashed on the dash, and the car slowed down. I flipped on my turn signal and drifted onto the shoulder. When I turned the key in the ignition to restart the car, nothing happened. No engine turnover, no battery click. Just silence.

Before you think this was a typical car breakdown story, it is not. This breakdown was entirely my fault. For months, I'd seen the check oil light on the dash, but I kept telling myself, "It's just a precaution—

the light comes on before it's actually needed." I was a broke college student, so I kept putting off the oil change.

Turns out, I put off the oil change for WAY too long. So long in fact that the car had run completely out of oil. Did you know that a car needs oil, like *needs* oil, to operate? After waiting for a tow to a nearby shop and hitching a ride down to Tucson with my boyfriend (now husband), I found out a few days later that I busted an engine rod and cracked the block. The car was totaled.

Here's the kicker: The reason I was even driving the car to Tucson was because I had just bought a new one. The car had belonged to my grandma, who'd passed away a few years earlier, and I was bringing it down so my sister would have a car to drive. Not only did I ruin my sister having a car, but I also destroyed something that meant a lot to my dad. Furious doesn't even begin to describe it. That weekend with my parents was tense. I apologized over and over again.

Back at school, I called the auto shop to see if anything could be done. They had no options for me—just a question: "When are you picking up the car?" I was a Resident Assistant living in a dorm, I had no money, no storage. Yet they informed me that every day the car sat at their shop, I'd be charged $100.

In a panic, I called my parents. What would you have done as a parent in this situation? Bailed your kid out? I probably would have, which would have placed the problem's solution squarely on me and added a bunch of stress to my life.

That's not what my dad did. I remember it clearly—my whole body flooded with cortisol. He said, "You did it. You need to deal with it."

End of story. Completely unmoved, no matter how much I begged or pleaded.

When I hung up that phone, I was furious.

WHAT BOUNDARIES ARE

On an episode of *Armchair Expert*, Dr. Becky Kennedy defined boundaries in a way I'd never heard before.[27] She said, "Boundaries are not something that you force other people to do. Boundaries are what you will do."

You know the typical response when someone does something and you may say, "You need to respect my boundaries and leave the room!" That's not a boundary. That's just telling someone what to do.

My dad set a boundary by refusing to help me figure out what to do with the car. He would not step in. He would not assist. I was left to do it by myself. I was so mad at him. And yet, it was the biggest confidence builder of my entire life.

He protected his time and sanity, as well as demonstrated that he had the confidence in me that I could figure it out myself—at least that's what I took from the situation years later.

I tell you this because other people's emotions are one of the reasons we hesitate to set a boundary. We fear the other person will blow up and we're afraid of being seen as a bitch or unreasonable. I want you to know that *yes*, in the moment all those things could happen. It's part of the process. It's part of letting go and letting other people have

27 Dr. Becky Kennedy (clinical psychologist and author), *Armchair Expert with Dax Shepard*, episode "Dr. Becky Kennedy (psychologist on parenting)," November 16, 2023, Wondery.

their emotions and reactions. **Those emotions and reactions aren't your responsibility.**

HOW TO GET BETTER AT SETTING BOUNDARIES

Perhaps it's our inclination—or social conditioning as people pleasers—but I find that many women have an incredibly hard time setting boundaries. You might fear social exclusion if you say no. For example, if you decline another request to volunteer at school, you might worry that you won't be invited to chaperone the field trip. It's as if we feel obligated to say yes to everything so we don't get shut out of the things we actually want to do.

I call it malarky. Setting boundaries is a way for you to protect your own energy and mental health. I have a few tips if you have trouble setting a boundary.

Define your values

Yes, we talked about this in the last chapter—but it bears repeating. Knowing your values gives you a grounded, logical way to say yes or no in the moment.

Anne, a mom from Connecticut and Balance member, ran into an issue at home. She loved her space neat and decluttered. One day, she and her husband spent a few hours organizing their laundry room. By the end, Anne felt inspired—energized to keep going. Her husband, on the other hand, was done.

Two of Anne's core values are freedom and connection. She enjoys decluttering because it gives her the freedom to live on her terms. But because she also deeply values connection, she often defers to what her husband wants.

She told me, "After dinner, I suggested we pick *one* small area to clean out. And he said 'Sure.' Before, I would have given in to what he wanted and been frustrated and resentful. I clearly stated what I wanted and we're both happy."

All this to say, when you know your values, you can figure out the true reasons for your actions and reactions and are thus better equipped to pursue activities that truly fuel your happiness.

Recognize your emotions

Resentment is a common emotion many moms on the edge of burnout feel. It shows up when we're doing something we think we should do, but don't actually want to. Learning to spot the early signs of resentment can be the difference between calmly saying no in the moment or losing your temper later on. I've learned to recognize resentment in my body after doing too many things I didn't want to do, and then having what seemed to others like overblown reactions. For me, that usually meant screaming at walls and slamming doors.

The first time I said no to avoid one of these reactions was with my daughter. I had offered that day to help her wash her comforter on her bed, thinking that when she asked, it would be sometime in the next few hours.

At 10:00 p.m. that night, she came into my room while I was in bed reading and asked for help with her comforter. Old me would've said, "Well, I did promise to help..." But then I fast-forwarded in my mind to what that "help" would actually look like.

I'd throw the covers off and snap, "Fine!" Then stomp down the hall, avoid eye contact, and roughly toss the sheets and comforter into the washing machine. I'd slam the lid shut and stomp back to bed. Minutes later, I'd feel like absolute crap for how I'd acted and have to apologize.

It occurred to me—I could avoid all of that by just saying no. Of course, my daughter countered with, "But you promised!" I held my ground: No. She stomped away, angry—and that's fine. Her frontal lobe isn't fully developed. Her reaction was completely normal.

Because I was able to recognize the little tendrils of resentment forming, that reaction didn't have to be mine.

Act (or don't act)

My husband always reminds me that "No" is a complete sentence. But is it—when it comes to setting boundaries? I think it works in some situations. If it's a request you've already said no to many times, then no further explanation is needed because you've already explained.

But "Hi, I'm JoAnn and I'm a boundary pusher." If someone tells me no to something that I've already convinced myself I want, I will not accept that boundary immediately. I will inquire. I will ask why and I'll want to know exactly why the no was said, especially when I don't feel like I'm being told the complete truth.

Because of this, I can't be surprised. My husband has tried to plan birthday surprises, but I always find out because I push boundaries until I'm satisfied. I used to think this was a character defect (because that's what I was told), but I don't anymore. My brain immediately picks out when "one of these things is not like the other" (shoutout to my fellow Sesame Street generation) and I feel uneasy until I know why.

So, if you've got boundary pushers like me in your life, when you say no, also say why. It doesn't have to be elaborate. "Because I don't want to" is perfectly acceptable. And then, don't do it.

THE TOTALED CAR

Your boundaries, even though potentially uncomfortable to set at the time, can make such a difference in the other person's life for the better. They may find out who they are and what they're capable of as a result of you not stepping into help, particularly if it's a boundary that you're setting with your kids.

When I hung up the phone with my dad, I was scared. I could already see how leaving the car in that shop in Casa Grande would drain my bank account in three days or less. I had to come up with a way out.

Thankfully, something interesting had happened to me the previous summer. I was a summer session RA, about to get in my car outside my dorm, when campus police pulled up behind me. Like most people, I had an immediate rush of fear. What did I do? Did I park wrong? But no—when the officer got out, he started admiring my car. "I've been looking for a car like this. If you ever plan on selling it, here's my card." I kid you not. Luckily, I'd held onto that card, and that's who I called.

He agreed to drive down to the shop in Casa Grande to take a look. He loved the car and wanted to restore it, so he made me an offer: $200 to buy it—which was generous, considering the car was now useless. He'd also cover the fees to get it out of the shop.

I took the deal—grateful, relieved, and proud that I'd found a way out of what could've been a very expensive mess.

TAKE ACTION

Is there a situation right now in which you can feel the seeds of resentment building? If so, it may help you to say no and set a strong boundary about what you will and won't do.

Picture your reaction if you don't set the boundary:

- Will you act in a way you are proud of?
- Will you feel supported or will you feel taken advantage of?

Reflect on these when considering if you should say no or not.

PERMISSION SLIP

If you feel that resentment building, give yourself permission to say no. Think of all the future apologies you won't have to make.

Next, we're digging into one last mindset that becomes an issue for many moms. As a result of focusing on our kids' needs for years, we forget what we ourselves want out of life. Let's dig into how to fix that.

CHAPTER 15

"My Kids Are My Whole World."

Our job as parents is to work ourselves *out* of a job. We want to raise kids who are independent, confident, and capable. Knowing that we won't have this time intensive parenting role forever, it's smart and positive role-modeling for your kids to have a life outside of them, their needs, and their activities.

Allow me to get a little feisty. I was at a happy hour with my friends, who I feel very comfortable sharing my true feelings with. We were sitting outside at a local place called Freeley's. For the past half hour, the conversation had been all about everyone's kids—what summer programs they were doing, what colleges they were eyeing, what drama was unfolding. Yawn. I was bored.

I know most of these kids and I enjoy getting an update, but to me, it had reached a point where that was all we were talking about. What happened to our lives? What happened to our goals?

I interrupted the conversation, "That's it. No more talk about the kids. I want to know what exciting things are happening just for you."

My friend Shana jumped in with her next planned trip (she's a travel agent and goes *everywhere*). But then the conversation steered back to where everyone's kids wanted to go. I gave up.

Does this happen to you around other adults? All the attention and exciting changes belong to the kids. I always think, "As kids, why were we so excited to become adults and do fantastic things when all we now talk about is our kids?"

Even saying this out loud sparks a flicker of guilt. I love my kids, don't get me wrong. They're amazing, and if I wanted to talk about them, I'd have no shortage of material. But I also feel a responsibility to not make them my whole world. They need me to be an emotionally stable rock—someone far enough removed from the ups and downs in their lives that when they come to me with a problem, I don't fall apart. Why does this help? Because the issue doesn't immediately disrupt my entire world. I have my own life so that I can be that emotional support for them without falling apart.

I recently started mountain biking, and there's a concept in the sport called rider-bike separation. When you're on a trail, there are rocks and bumps that can be brutal if you're planted flat in your seat. But you're not. Your feet are in a horizontal, level pedal position—so you don't snag your bottom foot or tip the bike going over hills. You keep equal pressure in each foot, with your bottom hovering just above the seat. That way, your legs—the strongest part of your body—absorb the impact, instead of your spine, which isn't built for that kind of pounding.

Think about that in relation to your kids. With my bike, I'm still part of the ride, but I've positioned myself to handle all the bumps and divots in the trails without being permanently damaged by them. That's the kind of separation I urge you to have with your kids. That's what this entire book has been leading toward.

HOW TO SEPARATE MY LIFE FROM MY KIDS

It comes down to four main areas: What you feel, what you say, what you hear, and what you see in your future. Sound familiar? This is exactly what I introduced in the beginning of this book and what we've been working through. The key is learning to protect each of these with strong boundaries. Here's what that looks like in practice.

Calming your reaction

I used to feel significant stress if one of my kids experienced stress, whether it was friend drama or they were feeling sick. I'd ruminate on how I could help or fix something for them. Since I was so preoccupied with my own kids, my emotional capacity was reduced to zero for other events, whether it was work or friend related.

Controlling my own stress has been the first step in working to become a non-reactive presence to my kids' emotions. Remember in Chapters 2 and 3, how we worked on circle thinking and Mind, Body, Unicorn Time? This is how you can become aware of your physical reaction and take the steps to calm yourself down.

By noticing and calming my own physical reaction, I've been able to remain present and reasonable so that I can see problems for what they are and not rely on my intense emotional response.

Explaining my own needs

When my kids were younger, I'd be alone with them from school pickup until seven or eight p.m. every night. Having kids is hard. Your stress levels rise, your body is drained from the day, and yet you're expected to enjoy every second of it.

It's the perfect recipe for guilt, stress, and shame. And here's the thing—it's not new. This kind of stress has always existed for moms. Decades ago, physicians prescribed "Mommy's Little Helper"—Valium, a muscle relaxant—for exactly this kind of overwhelm. Imagine how much easier those long afternoons would've felt physically with the help of something that relaxed your entire nervous system.

All of this is to say: Your stress is real. It's not in your head. You're not making a big deal out of nothing, and you're not bad at handling things. You're just carrying more than anyone ever admits. This is really hard. As women, we've been taught to ignore what we're feeling and just push through, which leads to extra stress, resentment, and blowups. Because we're pushing through, we start expecting the same from everyone else. And when those expectations aren't met, we step in and do it ourselves. Ultimately, creating more distance from the people we love.

Sometimes it seems easier to do it yourself than to step in and put up a fight. I'm speaking from experience. You have a voice in you that tells you when you're upset about a situation, and you've trained yourself to ignore it. When you acknowledge that, you'll find that all the anger is not a personal shortcoming. It's not that you can't go with the flow or be nicer. Your anger is telling you that something needs to change because it's affecting you.

There's one caveat. Sometimes, we make assumptions about other people's behavior that aren't true—and it's the assumption that sparks the reaction, not the behavior itself. There have been countless times I've been mad at my husband for staying at work late and "leaving me" to deal with the kids. He thought I was worried about his safety, something he couldn't control. But I wasn't. I felt abandoned. I felt like he was choosing work and office responsibilities over me.

After speaking with him, I realized my anger reflected an assumption I had about the situation - not what actually happened. Once he knew the reason behind my anger, he started to pay more attention to the time and communicate clearly when he planned to come home.

Or the times I've felt angry at a friend for snapping or being short, only to find out later that she was dealing with something heavy at home she hadn't shared. As soon as I know the real reason, the anger fades.

Being able to ask the questions necessary to uncover the person's point of view is key to actually understanding how you feel about the true situation, not the made up one in your head. I say that with all the kindness because I am the queen of making up situations in my head.

Have your own goals

I was at a doctor's appointment the other day when my provider asked about my daughter. I launched into updates—everything going on in her life—until I stopped myself. This was about to become another conversation about my kids. I am an interesting person too. I have to remind myself of that all the time.

I brought up my book—this book you are right now reading. I said I almost finished the rough draft and I was excited about it. People's expressions change when you go from talking about your kids to saying something cool you're doing. I think because it's so rare that adults do that. They get excited for you. An energy returns to the conversation that felt so routine before.

And you get excited again. All the nerves of putting yourself out there—the risk of it not working—come rushing back. It's uncomfortable, but it's glorious.

Focusing on your own thing takes the pressure off your kids too. Their wins and losses don't feel so personal anymore, because they're not. The victory or failure is theirs alone. You can still cheer them on or comfort them when they fall, but now you're emotionally available in a different way. You're not reacting from your own stress or identity. You're just showing up with love, and that makes your support so much deeper.

Having boundaries

Finally, after being able to control your stress levels, communicate effectively, and have your own goals, you put the boundaries in place to protect it all. Think of boundaries as what you're going to do or not going to do.

If your teen forgets to unload the dishwasher and you see dishes piling up in the sink, a boundary would be to let them stay there and not do it yourself. There are other ways to enforce chores than stepping in and doing them for your kids.

You have power and control over your life. You don't have to do something just because someone else is upset. Your job is not to make everyone else happy. You only have control over your own happiness, and the best mom is a happy mom.

TAKE ACTION

You've reached the end and now have the building blocks to take control of your own life instead of only reacting to what your kids and family want.

Use that lotus flower we discussed at the beginning of this book as your roadmap. The flower has five petals which represent:

1. Becoming aware of where you're starting and your current challenges. You can rise up from wherever you are now, regardless of your past actions or behaviors.

2. Gaining more control over your own stress through enriching Mind, Body, Unicorn Time.

3. Practicing active listening and questioning to improve what you hear and what you say.

4. Finding your own DREAM goal and going after something just for you.

5. Protecting what you create with firm boundaries.

Give yourself permission to be your own person, especially since you're a mom. Your kids' successes and failures are not your own and when you separate yourself, you can be better available to them emotionally.

You met me at the beginning of this book when I was crying on the couch on Christmas day. After putting these changes in place, let me show you what life looks like now.

CHAPTER 16

Conclusion

The Christmas I broke down, I had taken on all the responsibility for the entire holiday, thinking that my husbands' work schedule was too much on him.

The following Christmas, my husband took over all gifts and it's been that way ever since. On Christmas morning, I sometimes don't even know what my kids will be unwrapping. While that was a guilt hurdle at first, I now think it's glorious. I love not having to organize wish lists. Instead, I get to make food and invite family over, which I love since one of my values is connection.

My question to you now is: Where are you holding on to too much? Where can you let go so that other people can have a chance to step in and help you out? Move forward. Take imperfect action. Start the conversation with your partner (if you have one) or with your kids about how you will step back from specific things so that they can step forward.

A few ideas of things kids can take ownership of are:

- Remembering to do their homework
- Packing their own lunch
- Making sure pets get fed
- Cleaning up after themselves at mealtimes

Most of all, I want you to know that you don't have to do everything to be a good mom. You are enough as you are. Accepting other people's help is not a sign of weakness or ineptitude. You're exhibiting strength when you let others step in. You're showing your kids how to work as a team. That's powerful.

I no longer dread December because I took stock of my stress levels, communicated with my husband and kids, knew my own values, and put up boundaries about what I would and would not do. That's what I want for you too.

Remember, the best mom is a happy mom. Take care of you, and go take that imperfect action.

ACKNOWLEDGEMENTS

This book felt hard to sit down, focus and write. Starting body doubling with my Balance community helped me immensely so I want to thank all the women who showed up at 6AM to work on their own goals alongside me: Christy, Brittany, Allie, Donna, Kim. Mariekris, Kellie, Nancy & Anne.

Thank you to all my Lolas in Balance who trust me and put the skills and framework that I explain in this book into practice in their own lives. Your success is the biggest joy to me!

Thank you to Christina Gabrielle who was the first to read this book in full and catch all my inconsistencies. I greatly appreciate your time and your incredible eye for detail.

Thank you to Brie Tucker who celebrated me every time I sat down to write 1200 words. You helped me keep going.

Thank you to my friends and people I interviewed in the Happy Mom Summit and the No Guilt Mom podcast. I learn so much from your stories and experiences.

Thank you to my own mom who helps ground me through all the ups and downs of motherhood. I love you.

A huge thank you to my husband who is my constant sounding board and encouragement. And thank you to my kids who make this work so important. You're the ones I try the hardest to be a happy mom for.

READ MORE:

DREAD HOMEWORK TIME?

"This is the best book I have read on how to help your child with homework!"

- DHamon, Amazon Review

WANT YOUR KIDS TO HAVE BETTER FRIENDSHIPS?

"This was a lifeline for us. I was able to read it with my daughter and we began to relate better."

- C. Barefield, Amazon Review

JoAnn Crohn, M. Ed is a parenting educator and certified life coach who helps moms become happier and more connected parents by prioritizing themselves.

She's an accomplished writer, author, podcast host of the award winning No Guilt Mom Podcast, and speaker, appearing in national media and founder of the company, No Guilt Mom. Her specialty is helping moms go from martyr to model - being the role model in her family vs. sacrificing their own needs. Her coaching program Balance has helped hundreds of women find what lights them up, form a deeper relationship with their families and release their own mental load.

JoAnn is a former elementary school teacher with a Master's degree in Education as well as a National Board Certified Teacher. She's a mom to 2 kids.. She married her college sweetheart and they live in Gilbert, AZ.

URGENT PLEA!

Thank You For Reading My Book!

I really appreciate all of your feedback and
I love hearing what you have to say.

I need your input to make the next version of this

Please take two minutes now to leave a helpful review on
Amazon letting me know what you thought of the book.

Thank you!

JoAnn